I0586631

Pangyrus

Pangyrus © 2019
All Stories © 2019
Attributed to the authors named herein, except when noted otherwise
under "Acknowledgements"
ISBN: 978-0-9979164-4-7

All rights reserved
Printed in the United States of America
First published in 2019

For information about permission to reproduce selections from this book,
please write to Permissions at info@pangyrus.com

The text of this book is set in Palatino
with display text set in Crimson and Baskerville
Composition by Abraar Chaudhry
Cover design by Doug Woodhouse

Editor: Greg Harris
Managing Editor: Cynthia Bargar
Print Edition Manager: Susan Wyssen
Fiction Editors: Anne Bernays, Erica Boyce Murphy
Poetry Editor: Cheryl Clark Vermeulen
Nonfiction Editor: E.B. Bartels
Food Writing Editor: Deborah Norkin
Science Editor: Mona Tousian
Comics Editor: Dan Mazur
Contributing Editor: Sarah Colwill-Brown
Reviews Editor: Chris Hartman
Special Projects Editor: Virginia Pye
Graphic & Web Designer: Esther Weeks
Social Media: Yahya Chaudhry, Delea Mowatt
Readers and Copy Editors: Dee Costello, Chris Hartman, Molly Howes,
Jess McCann, Robert Olechna, Kelsey Pereira
Editorial Assistant: Suzannah Lutz
Logo Design: Ted Ollier
Pangyrus
79 JFK Street, L103
Cambridge, MA 02138
pangyrus.com

Contents

Fiction and Comics

Pangyrus

Note from the Editor

The act of protest that launched Protestant Christianity, Martin Luther's nailing of his 95 theses to the door at Wittenberg in 1517, usually gets framed as a story of spiritual life: theological purification confronting institutional corruption. And surely it was that. Luther protested, among other things, the sale of Indulgences, church documents that in the late Middle Ages allowed a new urban, moneyed class to buy their way out of Purgatory.

With the advent of printing, suddenly Indulgences were everywhere. Most of us know that Johannes Gutenberg, famed inventor of printing in Europe, introduced his Bible to the market in 1455. Fewer know that this was his second product. To help fund the holy book, he printed a 1454 Plenary Indulgence. For the next half century and more, Indulgences became major money-makers for printers and the Church alike.

This cheapening through proliferation is, perhaps, the usual story we tell ourselves of the internet. We indulge ourselves in clickbait and, half-hypnotized, half-irritated, forget what we read a moment after we've read it--or, worse, imprint indelibly in our memories that video of a cat boxing an alligator. But what if the story of the internet is actually spiritual?

Author Keith Scribner proposes the following test for how to recognize literature that's actually worth your while: "Would my life be diminished, had I not read it?" So much of what we indulge in, day to day--the Twitter outrages, the third bit of commentary on the fourth episode of a TV series, the overselling of sex—fails that test.

Our aim, at Pangyrus, is to ace it.

We offer a different kind of indulgence. That of the reader settling in to enjoy the play of the mind, the opening of emotions. "What on earth could be more luxurious than a sofa, a book, and a cup of coffee?" writes Anthony Trollope. Alberto Manguel, in *A Reading Diary*, notes: "Maybe this is why we read, and why in moments of darkness we return to books: to find words for what we already know." But this is only half the power of reading: words, whether in print or online, can also bring us new experience.

Pangyrus Six brings you deep into rural America, into the cadences of the auctioneer in Guinotte Wise's poem "Farm Sale," memorializing a disappearing past and the loss of a family farm and the memories kept in old radios. It takes you to hipster Brooklyn in Vincent Yu's "The Asshole," where irony and ambition and the blighted economy curdle post-graduate life into the quest for social-media-ready acts of cruelty. To the seaside of South Florida, where elderly Holocaust survivors arrange pool aerobics and grilled cheese against the threats of a chaotic world.

You'll visit the edges of American modernity, where in Joshua Shapiro's "Shooting Pool" server farms meet gun culture. And travel deep into the interior of human struggles. Claire Chafee's "Birdwatching" wrestles with the profound betrayal of an act of self-protection; Erin Pushman's "Through the Windshield" with the terrible innocence of not even knowing to protect yourself. Kendra Stanton Lee's "All in for Milli Vanilli" reveals the canned performances we play for others, and what it takes to speak in an authentic voice. Mike Sinert's "Butterfly" shows how long, and how costly, the struggle for redemption can be. And Vera Krom's "Icarus, in Old Age" dramatizes how a calling can be "a severing/ of every ligature/ your world has spun you."

This issue introduces a new focus on science, with Benoît Rey's window-rattling polemic, "Our Lies Are Our Fondest Hopes," and Alex Ahmed's "Political Machines," in which high-tech's utopian promises meet our ongoing, human failures of intent and will.

Pangyrus Six also launches *Zest!* for food writing. *Zest!* editor Deborah Norkin, in "Liver and Onions," finds her mother through food; Dariel Suarez, in "Father's French Fries," identifies the magic where memory and taste meet. Marley Stuart in "Good Fortune" gives us the flavor of wish fulfilment in the form of peach strudel.

There are many more pieces we could highlight, but--an introduction that hangs around too long onstage is no welcome at all. Everything in here is highlights, pieces that have won the hearts of editors. Read, enjoy! More than that: we hope you will walk away feeling that this art--to quote Keith Scribner again--"expands us and deepens us, as life's big experiences do."

—Greg Harris

With special thanks to Susan Wyssen, our new print edition manager (and co-editor of this note, though not this part, which would be weird), Cynthia Bargar for managing the unmanageable, Deborah Norkin for whipping together the food writing, Anne Bernays and Erica Boyce Murphy for fiction, Cheryl Clark Vermeulen for her astonishing and intrepid eye for poems, E.B. Bartels for nonfiction, Dan Mazur for comics, Mona Tousian for science editing, and the whole crew of volunteers who make Pangyrus possible!

Liver and Onions

by Deborah Norkin

*I*n third grade, I was assigned as homework to prepare my favorite meal for my family. I chose to make liver and onions. An odd selection for an eight-year-old, but my experience with food was limited. My mother's spice cabinet contained salt, paprika, dried minced onions and garlic powder. When I first saw an actual head of garlic, I remember being surprised. I had assumed that garlic, like salt, came only in shaker form.

Feeding our family, which my mother unfailingly did, was not her favorite thing. Between work, kids, and keeping the house going, she was always in a rush. She broiled everything because it was fast: chicken legs with leathery skin, steaks done past well, and hamburgers with no hint of pink. Broiled liver was special. That, she smothered under a heaping mountain of sautéed onions.

So together we peeled and sliced, then slid the onions into nearly smoking oil. She handled the slippery slab of calf liver and flipped it after ten minutes to ensure a consistent chewy texture. She did most of the work, but when we ate, she praised me for my contribution. I was as proud as if I'd done it all.

Something about the transformation from raw ingredients to meals spoke to me. By high school, my mother became my sous chef. If I said, "Chop," she asked, "How small?" I planned our weekly menu and we shopped for food together. My mother was thrilled to offload the chore and, I now suspect, spend time with her usually cranky teenager. I couldn't, or to be honest, wouldn't talk to my mother about things that were going on in my adolescent and young-adult life. I'm sure she had her own private struggles but no matter what we faced in each of our lives, preparing a meal together was wonderfully ordinary. Chop, cook, eat, clean, repeat.

For her, a learning disability made translating written instructions into action a tortuous endeavor. My ability to interpret recipes and transform ingredients into meals was magic to her. Her ability to pick up a bag of flour and estimate, within a tablespoon, how much was left was magic to me. She marveled as my skills improved, and my recipe repertoire moved to delicate butter sauces and soufflés. I marveled at how she fit every plate and bowl in the dishwasher and how, even at a crowded table, she always found room for one more.

If daily meals were not my mother's forté, cooking for crowds was. My mother collected people. New to the synagogue? Come for dinner. No place to go for Thanksgiving? There's plenty of soup. Menus were simple, but plentiful. She sectioned bushels of citrus for never-ending fruit salad. Tuna fish, deviled eggs, and always Margie's noodle kugel, a tribute to her dear friend who died of cancer at thirty-seven, the tragedy of which I didn't fully understand until I'd reached that age myself.

I think she was happiest when she hosted. Smiling, slightly harried, telling jokes, laughing, never stopping. It wasn't about the food for her. It was her way of showing she cared. Her reward was that moment when others understood they were important and special. She gave them that moment and in return received one of her own. When she fed others, she nourished herself.

From the very beginning, food was a bond between us. My mother nursed me and my sisters. It wasn't easy. Experts of the 1960s proclaimed science had improved upon nature but she chose to ignore them and gave herself to us in this most elemental way. She told us stories of breast feeding in bathrooms and how her own mother and sisters thought her ridiculous. One of my favorite pictures of her is a black and white snapshot. She is twenty-six and sitting in a car. Her head is tilted slightly to the side and her eyes are sleepy. Just out of frame is my newborn sister having breakfast.

In my family, we never spoke the words aloud. I said, *I love you* with chocolate-glazed profiteroles and creamy quiche with flaky crust. My mother said them back by buying me illustrated cookbooks and my first chef's knife. Over time, the number of knives in my canvas roll increased but there was always a special slot for that ten-inch blade with the black plastic handle that I carried to cooking school, to every restaurant I ever worked in, and back home again. I never imagined our time together would end so abruptly, but life, unlike a well-practiced recipe, is unpredictable.

When she was diagnosed with stage-four cancer at fifty-eight, all I could do was sit with her and hold her hand. Chemo made her nauseous and everything she ate tasted metallic. Then one day she asked for my pizza and my chocolate pudding and my homemade bread. I rushed home and turned out dish after dish. I wanted to care for her at the end of her life as she had cared for me at the beginning of mine.

At the hospital she took one bite of each then pushed them away. An oncology nurse told me it was common. Dying patients wanted to taste their favorite foods one last time. It helped them, she said, to make peace with what they were leaving behind. I had, irrationally, wanted what I'd desperately prepared to miraculously heal my mother. Instead, what I'd created helped her to say goodbye.

Now that I have a family of my own, I make sure to say the words but, like my mother, I show how much I love them. When my children were old enough, I taught them to cook. They use the knife my mother gave me forty years before. Though the steel is whittled and liver will never be on the menu, when they chop onions, I shed a tear, not because I'm sad, but because I see in them what my mother saw in me and, if they're very lucky, what they may someday see in children of their own.

Though she never met my two girls, I believe my children know my mother through the indelible lessons she instilled in me. Deeds speak louder than words, be generous and kind toward others and, maybe the most important and difficult lesson of all: Though love is infinite, time, regrettably, is not.

Farm Sale

by Guinotte Wise

The auctioneer is rhythmical, sounds like a country song
sometimes, staccato and hard-edged at others, always
insistent on ridding the farm of its last owner's life.
Cans of washers, Mason Jars, old tack from huge
horses that died working like the man who drove them.

God this guy is good, must be a livestock seller doing
a favor, he points, he gestures, the sound he makes is
hypnotic, call and response, my hand flies up, one money
on five old radios, whatamI whatamI bid eight now ten
nasal like Hank Snow, twenty now twentyfive biddem

thirtybidhupfortynowfortyheardfifty he never stops, no
breaks in his words, they flow like a code of religious
witchery that heals and makes you dance eyes roll back
chicken voodoo and snake church ecstasy a runaway
log truck but smooth like a sewing machine you just

can't describe well you know when a hard rain starts it
pulsates like that only danceable, better, I surrender to
the magick and buy five radios for one money twotwo
doIheartwotwentySOLDfortwohundred then it all quits
and his ringman gives him a bottled water and he lights

up a corktipped cigarette, and the crowd moves down
and I see the radios closer up, I paid too much but I am
exhilarated waiting for him to start up his hands moving

gracefully face expressionless eyes quick rap seems
slow and ponderous with this supernovastar, that good.

One radio played Wabash Cannonball or Orange Blossom
Special, I know this, and the couple danced in the kitchen
whirling on the linoleum, she breathless, he serious, and
I will restore it, make it play again, it will glow and hum
its Bakelite warm and we will dance, whirl on linoleum

He starts again hundiddyhummawhattamabidstainless
steel milkyercowsurgemilkerstartatTENhearfifteenhup
nowtwentyfive and the crowd is rapt and Buddy Rich's
drum solo Not So Quiet Please would fall and stumble
lag behind the rapidfire headlong arpeggio, the cadence.

Atlantic Grille

by Eliezra Schaffzin

I'm at the Atlantic Grille with my Great Aunts Helen and Matil-
da. We're having grilled cheese sandwiches, the only item on
the menu they'll eat, the only one they'll pay for. The Atlantic Grille
serves the four towers of their Florida condominium. It features
surf-and-turf on the Specials board and swim diapers in the dessert
case. We've taken our lunch out on the deck, overlooking the pool,
and beyond that, the beach. My aunts are quiet, munching, staring
off into the perfectly deep-blue sky where it meets perfectly pale-
blue water. I can see the dip in the sand where, early this morn-
ing, I strode ungracefully into the ocean. At that hour, the beach
was empty of people, the pool empty of everyone but Helen and
Matilda, who marched back and forth in opposite directions, two
sentries on the ramparts, their kerchiefed heads just clearing the
surface of the shallow end. Now every inch of the pool is occupied
by a water aerobics class ("the usual mermaids and one merman,"
I hear the instructor say). The empty space where I swam out be-
fore, my heartbeat quickening at the vastness of my private bath, is
now dotted with the Russian Flotilla, the condominium's coalition

of former Soviets who speak only to each other and bob in the water for hours at a time. A man on a bicycle—young, black, barefoot, stout—navigates his way over the sand to the condo's concrete entryway, where he leans his bicycle against a stack of lounge chairs and from the pockets of his jeans produces a small plastic bottle and a large pink loofah. He strips to his boxers and steps under the shower just outside the condominium door. I catch the rise and fall of the aerobics instructor's voice, and then other voices: a sudden yelp, and then another, as if the merman has goosed a few 'maids. My aunts continue their faraway munching, but I lean forward in my seat for a better view of the pool. The instructor can't keep her students' attention: there's some kind of commotion, further cries of alarm. Irma from Turkey wades to the ladder, rises from the pool, and pads, dripping, over to Maria, who's just finished cleaning the men's bathroom. "There's a fish in the pool," Irma shouts. Maria nods, and pushes her mop into the ladies' room. Irma picks up the emergency phone. "There's a fish in the pool," I hear again, and then more cries from the water, some giggles. The teacher counts out an exercise beat at the top of her lungs, while two Russian husbands brush past her, very close, and descend the stairs to the beach, aiming to join the flotilla. They go no further than the shower: soon there's more shouting, in differently accented English. The young man stands very still under the running water, pink loofah in one hand, shower gel in the other. Three more Russian husbands break from the flotilla and trudge up the beach, sea water glistening on their tanned, seventy-something chests. My aunts' gaze refocuses sharply to the immediate foreground as two uniformed men pass our table: the first carries a long metal implement, a hook at one end, a net at the other; the second holds a hefty contraption that makes me think of generators and jump starts. On the table the Atlantic Grille's thick paper napkins ball up tightly inside arthritic hands. My own pulse has again quickened, and my mind translates its message: What are they going to do to him? To my pulse's message, my mind responds, as it always does, What are you talking about? I look to the beach. Offshore, the flotilla reconstitutes itself. The young man is gone, though I detect his soapy footprints in the sand; his bicycle still leans by the lounge chairs. As the uniformed pair approaches the pool, the ladies let out a cheer: the merman carries the culprit from the water in one hand. It's about eight inches long, silver, and completely still. It falls heavily into the first man's outstretched net. The second lays his strange apparatus at the instructor's feet, and as she pokes a triumphant finger at the power button, it announces itself as an outdoor stereo, conquering the scene with the sudden pounding of music. On the beach, the young man, fully dressed now, creeps back to retrieve his bicycle. He rides off unsteadily across the sand as the stereo lets out a booming *aaaaaah-ya!* and a mambo launches the bodies in the pool into synchronized motion.

For dessert, my Great Aunts Helen and Matilda will have coffee ice cream: not here at the restaurant, but in Helen's kitchen, where she will shuffle to the freezer, lower a heavy box to the table, and serve herself and her sister in effortful scoops spread atop fragile wafer cones. In Auschwitz, Helen hid her black bread rations and fed them to Matilda in the dark, trying to ease her nausea. Matilda says her stomach was never very strong. Helen says her taste for food is dwindling. They don't even really like the sandwiches at the Atlantic Grille. But they love ice cream, and eat it in hearty, jealous bites, floor-to-ceiling blinds half closed, so that only sunshine and the great Atlantic penetrate the room through vertical lines: an empty, quiet paradise of perfect blue.

All in for Milli Vanilli

by Kendra Stanton Lee

All or Nothing is the name of Milli Vanilli's debut album. I am all in for Milli in 1989, and the fulfillment of my fourth grade wish will be a neatly wrapped cassette tape under the tree.

My mom lamented earlier this month that she hoped Santa will feed my baby brother Michael a bottle in the middle of the night. "He might as well, since he'll be up anyway," she sighed. I read between the lines. My mom is tired of waking up with an 18 month-old and she is tired of keeping up the Santa charade for a 9 year-old.

I let go of my rein on the mythical man as an act of mercy to my poor, tired mom.

***

Several cassette tapes are batched together in a present on Christmas morning. As I tear open the paper for the reveal, I think for a beat how these got here. How my dad probably bopped around the Sam Goody store in his freshly polished Johnston &

Murphy tasseled shoes, asking some unsuspecting teenage clerk where to find a "Vanilla Milli" or some errant nomenclature. But it's here, the oft-desired Milli cassette, and I am winning the fourth grade. *Girl you know it's true.*

***

On Christmas Day, we lounge around in our pajamas until my Nana comes over for dinner. Her annual ecstasy over the desserts and complaints over the pesky draft in every room are as much a tradition as Bing Crosby on the radio. My sister Taryn and I are permitted to sleep at the foot of the Christmas tree, snuggled in our brand new pastel sleeping bags. Taryn's has a rockin' California Raisin on the front. The tree is aglow, we have each consumed 4 pounds of homemade Christmas cookies today, and there is a Democratic majority in Congress. 1989 is a sublime time to be alive in Bay Village, Ohio. I fall asleep listening to Milli in my Walkman. I love how the B side triggers the tape player to turn off automatically.

Taryn and I spend the rest of Christmas break in our basement that smells like all Midwestern basements smell: a little like furnace, a little like flood. We choreograph a dance number to every Milli Vanilli song by week's end. Ironically we lip-synch to it so much the cassette tape eventually unravels; we don't know yet that Milli Vanilli's career will unravel similarly, for the same offense. Our dad asks us which one is Milli and which one is Vanilli. We groan a requisite groan.

Our mother takes us ice skating, while baby Michael stays with our grandparents. Our lawyer daddy clicks through the halls in his Johnston & Murphies and mock-whines that he doesn't have a Christmas break from his court appearances. He comes home after dinner and tells us stories in the dark about an idyllic childhood spent riding Red Schwinn bicycles and restitching leather baseball gloves. My parents orchestrate magical holidays for us. Sometimes their Christmases Past are woven into our Christmas Present. I have no fear for Christmas Future.

I even have my own Christmas Past on reserve. I have watched hours of our highlight reel on VHS cassettes, which my mother captures in wobbly spurts with her video camera. Although 1989 is the peak of compact Sony camcorders, my dad has recently purchased my mom a video camera the size of a baby water buffalo at an independent establishment called Tapes-to-Go. It is a tiny shop nestled in our little suburban hamlet where one rents movies on VHS, and where one can also purchase all manner of electronics including television sets, VCRs, turntables and, evidently, video cameras. There is an economy to Tapes-to-Go that is known in Bay Village and I assume everywhere. You have to be quick on the draw if you want a newly released movie. Returning VHS tapes without having rewound them is a near-capital offense, punishable by heavy fines.

My mom keeps stacks of our own family video tapes shelved and labeled, "Vacation," "Nora's Wedding," and "Christmas 1989." I can watch as Michael turns one and tries root beer for the first time. I can visit Taryn at her First Communion party where she is cutting a huge floral sheet cake. I can hear my mousy voice open the new hot rollers on Christmas morning and watch as I run around the house doing a victory lap.

***

I don't watch these videos anymore. Not merely because they require jimmy-rigging a multi-pronged tape/DVD/baby water buffalo together in order to access them. I don't watch the videos because I don't need to. I know today that this fourth grade year is the end of my girlhood. Judging from much of the world's child population whose innocence is robbed by human traffickers and warfare and greed, I am lucky it lasted as long as it did.

***

Taryn and I return to school in a whole new decade. The boy who looks at me with heavy hazel eyes, who told me before Christmas break that he liked me suddenly starts to look a little dimmer in my eyes. I am tired of doing his reading comprehension homework for him. Plus I think he is eyeing Jessica B. in the other homeroom. I have trouble falling asleep at night. I oscillate between the *Cocktail* soundtrack and Milli Vanilli, who have just been nominated for a Grammy for best new artist.

In February, the lead singers of Milli Vanilli, Fab Morvan and Rob Pilatus, hug each other's dreadlocks as they accept the golden gramophone trophy. They give a shout-out to all the other artists in the audience and those watching at home. They tell them they can achieve what Milli Vanilli has achieved. They say, "This award is for all the artists in the world."

But in November, Milli Vanilli is stripped of its Grammy for the high crime of lip-synching. A couple months later, my parents tell us that they are separating. Both events, though unrelated, seem to strike a similar note. The music I was hearing was incorrectly labeled. I was mistaken. The singers' mouths were moving but the message I heard wasn't theirs.

Milli Vanilli, when interviewed about their cover being blown after a recording kept skipping while they performed live, describe wanting to die. Yet, their farce was choreographed from the beginning when they became the pretty puppets of unknown singers. I wonder how long they expected to be able to carry on the fraudulence. I wonder if they began to believe their own lies.

My parents' separation is temporary, but my faith in lasting things is shattered. I don't know how to process it all, because last year I wanted *All or Nothing* and this year I just want all of my family together under one roof. I don't want to talk about it at all. Also, I want to talk about it all the time but only with kids whose parents are also split up.

Taryn and I soldier on, bickering and borrowing clothes and still lounging around in our Midwestern basement, inventing dance routines inspired by music videos we watch on VH1. We do our best to support one another, but sometimes we escape to our quiet corners to listen to our mixtapes of sadness and confusion and grief. Years later, my parents do divorce. They are congenial toward each other and make endless sacrifices for their kids.

***

I grew up with considerable privilege and even during their separation and divorce, my parents ensured we had as much stability as possible. After college, I worked for years with at-risk youth, many of whom lacked the basic resources of food and shelter. One constant I have found, though, is that kids, no matter their socio-economic status, can become expert lip-synchers.

When your parents are going through a hard time, you learn how to memorize the song, the party line, the message that tells the story folks can handle. You start to build a muscle memory, your mouth forms around the words so well. The song may as well have been pre-recorded. You offer a chorus that'll stick in their heads. People ask how you're doing. I'm fine, things are good, you say, And you? Your response becomes a song you know by heart.

The song I learn to lip-synch is the antithetical *All or Nothing*. It is a soft ballad that concedes to having just enough of what I need and a little of what I want. I remember how much older I felt when adults asked me, in that sympathetic, expectant tone, how my parents were doing. I was glad to call upon the ready-made responses. My first taste of maturation was that no one was really saying what they meant.

***

In the spring of the year I left for college, Milli Vanilli recorded a so-called comeback album, B*ack and In Attack*. But Rob Pilatus was entangled in a whole net of troubles, drugs and assaults and rob- beries--oh my. The night before Milli Vanilli was supposed to leave for a promotional tour, Pilatus was found dead of an overdose in his German hotel room. The jury is still out on whether or not the overdose was a suicide. *Back and In Attack* was never released and the recordings may very well have been destroyed.

What a shame that Pilatus's legacy is tainted by the the harm he caused to himself and others, by the songs he didn't sing. But thankfully this isn't the end of the story. Because the other half of Milli Vanilli, Fab Morvan continued to go hard in music, DJ-ing and even releasing his own solo album. I listened to a more recent sin- gle he released, "Now You're Calling." It has a hot dance beat and the vocals are sort of pleasant and lulling like The Cure. You could imagine a lot of teens in Berlin crashing around to it in a dark Euro club. It made me smile to hear Morvan's real voice, his refined talent.

***

There was a moment early on in college when I realized the full lib- erty of not having to provide canned answers. A new friend in my dorm asked me how I felt about my family, about how everything shook out, and I felt free to say exactly how I was feeling. It took some practice but the gift of time and eventually a loving husband and all the Brene Brown books on vulnerability have net me a new song. I have written the song myself and I can sing it and believe every word because it's true. Sometimes I'm okay. Mostly, I'm okay. How are you?

I will not return to the VHS tapes but I will return to the Christmases Past in my mind's eye many times. Especially since now my children will sleep on that same floor at the foot of a now-fake Christmas tree in my mother's living room. Absent the smell of pine, the furnace is much quieter now since it's been replaced. My kids still wreck around in the same basement where Taryn and I ruined a Milli Vanilli tape. They descend to their lair to watch movies outside of my supervision. I tell them, "Don't forget to rewind," and they groan a requisite groan.

The Nutshell Studies of Unexplained Death

by Maryann Corbett

*Crime scene dioramas created as teaching tools by Frances
Glessner Lee, Renwick Gallery, Washington, D.C.*

Well-behaved voyeurs
bend above these exquisite
dollhouse miniatures

where the small-scale poor
die in '40s dailiness.
Blood speckles a floor

tiled in one-to-twelve
scale. Ditto bath fixtures, beds,
plates shocked from a shelf —

Here's a girl's sliced neck.
Here's another, legs jutting
from a tub, freaklike.

Is this Dresden head
brush-tipped with the purpling
livor of the dead?

To appreciate
such intently crafted pain,
one must contemplate

finger-cramping care:
quarter-inch-high postcards, penned
with a single hair,

a close eye for sin's
rigor vitae. Tiny socks
hand-knitted with pins.

Strict detail is key.
Rage, in grimy crevices:
Search for it and see,

sisters. As will I,
taken with the pains by which
quiet women die.

Granite

by Judy Kessler

Joyce Leblanc is standing at the central island of her kitchen, regretting her choice of white granite over the composite the contractor recommended. Smack in the middle a red splotch radiates, like a strange scar after botched surgery. Joyce blames the contractor for not sealing the granite properly, which became apparent when one of her husband's buddies knocked over a bottle of Merlot at last month's Super Bowl party. Now she has this unsightly stain to contend with. She can't make too much of a stink, though, because the contractor is married to Blondie, her best friend since grade school.

Joyce drags her KitchenAid Professional mixer to the middle of the island so she can't see the stain. She fits the Bluetooth earpiece over her left ear, as she always does before making her PTA calls. It's the same model her husband uses to talk with clients, and wearing it reassures Joyce that her job, supervising their 13- and 16-year-old children while serving as President of Norumbega Middle School Parent Teacher Association, is just as important as his.

"Blondie? It's Joyce." Not that Blondie wouldn't recognize her number—they are on each other's Frequent Caller list—but

Joyce was taught in her first job, Administrative Assistant to the Vice-President of Norumbega Five Cents Savings, to be profession-al in every interaction no matter how insignificant it might seem.

"I'm in the middle of a cut and blow dry. Can we make it quick?" Blondie runs the only decent hair salon in town. In the background Madonna sings "Don't Cry for Me Argentina," while a hair dryer hums backup.

"Just a friendly reminder that tomorrow's the Teacher Appre-ciation Luncheon. I'm counting on you to bring something special. Of course we're honoring the entire staff, but I especially want to thank Mrs. Farnsworth. Can you believe she was our teacher all those years ago, and now she's got our girls?"

There is a pause.

Joyce informs Blondie, "I'm making my pumpkin spice brown-ies. I know I gave you the recipe when they were such a hit last year, but of course you'll want to bring something else." As she says this, Joyce opens the dark cherry door to her pantry. She collects canned pumpkin, flour, cocoa, baking powder, cinnamon, nutmeg, cloves. Everything at her fingertips, exactly where she's filed it.

Madonna recedes. The dryer drones on.

"Blondie, you still there? We could use an entrée."

"Sure, Joyce, don't worry. I'll figure something out." A smid-geon louder, she calls, "Be with you in a minute, Liza."

Liza? That explains why Blondie's distracted. Liza's been a troublemaker since they were all together at Norumbega High, when she and that creep Eddy used to snort coke after school till Liza's father got wind of it. Later she'd dropped out of college and run off to Portland. There was a rumor she'd waitressed in a topless dive when Eddy got busted for dealing. Joyce shuddered, imagin-ing. When Liza got pregnant there was a lot of talk, everyone with an opinion on whether it was Eddy's kid or a one-night stand. No wonder the child was so weird.

Blondie speaks quietly into the phone. "Have you noticed any-thing strange about Jess lately?"

Joyce's daughter Jessica and Blondie's daughter Chloe are also, as her thirteen-year-old says, BFFs. Joyce appreciates this mirroring of the mothers' friendship, orderly like her pantry, everything in its place. She thinks hard, is unable to dredge up anything unusual. "She does close her door more. Adolescents need their privacy, you know. Probably primping for some boy."

"I hope you're right," says Blondie. Then she adds, "The girls are working on a science project at our place, something about growing beans under lights. Chloe asked if Jess could stay for sup-per."

Joyce would prefer the girls gather at her house under adult supervision. Still, this is a wholesome, worthy activity. How could she refuse? She tells Blondie she'll pick up Jessica at 8.

Blondie rushes back to her clients, while Joyce returns to her measuring cups and teaspoons. It's not her daughter she's been wor-rying about, it's her husband. Brian's been working so many hours these last few months. When she questions his evening absences he says, "How do you think I earn those bonuses?" Brian reminds her they'll need that extra cash for college soon. Brandon, their oldest, is at football practice, getting a ride home from a teammate after the guys go out for cheeseburgers, so Joyce will be alone for supper again. She's glad to be baking today. It instills confidence. If you fol-low the recipe carefully, everything comes out right, and everyone appreciates the results.

She pours most of the brownie batter into a 13-by-9 sili-cone-coated steel pan. Then, instead of sliding it into the oven she leaves it on the counter, rinses her hands, and mounts the mauve-carpeted stairs to her bedroom. In her bedside drawer, be-hind her old diaphragm, under a paperback edition of *Pride and Prejudice* she is certain neither her children nor her husband will ever read, is a sealed plastic bag. These are her healing herbs. The bag feels lighter than she recalls, but she hasn't touched it since last week so she dismisses any doubts. She carries her healing herbs downstairs, measures out two teaspoons, stirs them into the last of the brownie batter and spoons it into four muffin cups.

Now both pans go into the oven. She should clean up but resents her family abandoning her, so she leaves everything out for the moment. She sits at the counter, drinking a glass of Merlot because who cares now if it spills, checking Facebook and reading her e-mail. She follows a link the principal has sent to a report on classroom bullying and its evolution in teens' social media world, feeling obliged to read the report as it's the main topic at the next PTA meeting.

The muffin cups are done first. She resets the timer for the larger pan, fifteen minutes more, then eases a hot brownie out of the muffin tin and breaks it open, giving it a minute to cool before taking that first bite. Between the chocolate and pumpkin and all those spices, you can't guess what else is in there.

Joyce savors the rest of her brownie while thumbing through *Good Housekeeping*. She's wiping away a loose crumb when the land line rings in the living room at the other end of the house. She really should put all her ingredients away and wipe the counters clean, but she doesn't want to miss anyone's phone call. She's left so many messages today, all these mothers out working now that their kids are in school. Occasionally she wishes she were one of them; even her old job at the bank would be less solitary. But most days she's glad to be home. Though it occurs to her that if she brought in a few dollars herself, Brian wouldn't need to work such long hours.

The caller is not from her PTA list. It's some vendor she doesn't recognize, asking about fixing her garage door. Is this another thing Brian hasn't told her about? She doesn't remember him mentioning it, but her mind is becoming fuzzy and relaxed. She tells the vendor to call back later when her husband is home.

She hangs up and lies down on the sofa. She's earned this. The cushions are soft. The cat jumps onto her lap and she pets his back, enjoying the sense of him stretched out on top of her.

Joyce dreams of warm bodies. She's lying on the Caribbean beach where she and Brian honeymooned, only Brian isn't there. She has loosed her bikini top. Hot sand glitters in the sun. The waiter has brought a delicious drink, a fermentation of cocoa, spice, and rum. Or is it coca and rum? People are dancing to island music, Conga drums and those cowbell things. The beat is insistent, a ringing that won't go away. Something about it smells off, like the time they strayed from the tourist beach and discovered teenagers burning old tires.

Wait. That ringing is no cowbell. She rubs her eyes, feels thirsty, and realizes too late that the ringing is her oven timer. She has no idea when the buzzing began, how long she's been asleep. Before she can reach her hot pads, the stench of burnt chocolate assaults her. On the granite counter, the cat noses her bag of healing herbs, oblivious to Joyce's cry.

***

Blondie has just trimmed off the last of Liza's home dye job. It's very short now, but at least she'll look presentable. Blondie understands why this client is perpetually short on cash. When Liza first came back from Portland, broke and burdened with baby, Blondie cut her hair for free. She sympathizes with single moms. Her own mother's struggle to make ends meet after Blondie's dad left is a big piece of why the salon is so important to her. Still, she wonders what possesses women to do a crappy job coloring their own hair and then have to live with it for weeks or months. And bright blue, to boot! Liza's natural color is a striking raven, same as her kid Maddie. Blondie hasn't seen Maddie in the salon ever. But she's watched the child exit the school bus and walk the rest of the way alone.

Blondie swivels the chair so Liza can see how great she looks, and asks if she can snap a picture for the salon's Facebook page. "You should bring Maddie in too. Even if she wears her hair long, I can trim the frayed ends, give it some shape."

Liza glares at her in the mirror. "That's ballsy. Considering what your kid and that overgrown Barbie doll Jessica Leblanc are doing to Maddie."

Blondie suspends her mister mid-air. She wants to ask Liza why, if she feels this way about Chloe, she's here instead of at the Super Scissors that opened in the strip mall. But she holds her tongue. Everyone in this town talks, and Liza's got friends too. Blondie listens to everyone's gossip, but she's made it a policy to dispense only positive items, the kind of news that will grow her business. "What do you mean?" she asks.

Liza digs into the hip pocket of her jeans, retrieves her phone, and brings up a text-and-photo app Blondie's never heard of. It seems Blondie's daughter has a different sharing policy than her mother. Somehow, Chloe or Jess, she's not sure who, has posted a shot of Maddie in the girls' locker room, arms crossed over her pancake breasts. Liza says the whole class has seen it.

Lately, when Chloe and Jess hide their phones, Blondie assumes they're stalking that boy who walked them home last week, a youth still croaking like a backyard frog. She thinks of notes Mrs. Farnsworth confiscated, decades ago, when Blondie would slip them to Joyce. The folded paper fortune teller where you'd lift up the corner to see who you'd marry, super-hot Brian Leblanc or that kid with the glasses who picked at his zits. Blondie wipes her hair-sprayed fingers on her smock, remembering what they used to say about Liza.

With Liza's permission, Blondie scans the rest of Chloe's posts. The newest is a photo of the science experiment. Jessica's reply hints they're growing more than lima beans under those fluorescents. Blondie has the urge to spray the phone with her mister but knows that won't help. She realizes now, this is why Liza's here. She's planned this moment to shock her, to enlist Blondie's aid in cutting this ugliness off at the root.

***

On her way to get Jessica, Joyce stops at the grocery and picks up a dozen frosted brownies for Teacher Appreciation Lunch. When she's home, she'll transfer them to her gold-rimmed wedding china platter. She also buys a half-dozen of those little cream puffs she loves. By the time she reaches Blondie's she has eaten three cream puffs, unaware of the crumbs that look like zits above her lip.

Blondie answers the door. "We need to talk," she says. But Joyce is not in any condition to talk. She tells her friend that Brian will be home for supper any minute, which she wishes were true. Chloe and Jessica descend from Chloe's room, giggling. Joyce adores their innocence.

Jessica seems especially cheerful as she snatches a cream puff from the open box and climbs into the back seat.

"I'm glad you're having fun with that science project," says Joyce. "Mrs. Farnsworth will be proud of you."

With her mouth full of cream puff, Jessica is hard to understand. Joyce hears something about a ship.

"Swallow your food, young lady."

"The sub said Mrs. Farnsworth broke her hip. She's having surgery and then rehab. She'll be out a couple of months."

Relief washes over Joyce. No one will judge her bringing store-bought brownies for a substitute, even after she's urged the other mothers to provide a home-made treat. It's too bad about Mrs. Farnsworth, but she's confident this experienced teacher has left excellent notes for the sub: lesson plans, tests, advice on handling troublemakers.

***

Teacher Appreciation Luncheon goes off without a hitch. Blondie comes through with a tray of lasagna from Rizutto's. Joyce's bakery brownies are a hit; only crumbs remain on her wedding china. Another parent offers to freeze any leftovers and take them to Mrs. Farnsworth while she's recuperating at home.

As the teachers enjoy their coffee and dessert, the principal, Dr. Martinez, thanks the PTA for providing this spread. Then she tells everyone about Mrs. Farnsworth's accident in case they want to send a card, and introduces the substitute, a middle-aged former waitress who earned her teaching certificate in a program for career changers, and who student taught in Jessica's class last year. The principal adds, "Some of you probably know her from her days at Rizutto's."

Joyce and Blondie wipe the tables after lunch, sponging up spilled tomato sauce that's overflowed the pan. Joyce would like to ask what her friend wanted to discuss last night, but now the substitute, the principal, and Liza, of all people, are heading their way. Despite her new haircut Liza looks grim, lips pressed in a line, though as they come closer, Joyce detects a gleam of satisfaction. Principal Martinez brandishes a cell phone, encased in pink with sequins and gold glitter. Joyce recognizes the case she gave Jessica for Christmas. She knows by heart its inscription: *Don't let anyone dull your sparkle.*

Blondie hisses, "Tried to warn you."

Joyce cannot imagine what warning is needed. Dr. Martinez and the substitute look like they're about to challenge a customer who tried to leave without paying his tab. They should show their appreciation for the nice lunch Joyce and her team have made. She thought the principal understood this.

Dr. Martinez directs Joyce and Blondie to two chairs in the corner. Only now does Joyce appreciate the principal's determination.

The PTA President sits, clutching her china plate to her chest, a fear sown in her that something's about to break.

***

Joyce can't think what to say to her daughter. The whole way home, the principal's words keep ringing in her ears: *You can't shove this thing back in the bottle.* Jessica slinks down in back, only her bangs visible in the rear view mirror. Dr. Martinez raised such a stink over a little picture, suspending both girls for three days, threatening legal consequences if the harassment doesn't stop. Warning they could be arrested if the girls are growing what Jess has implied.

Joyce would rather wait till Brian comes home to deal with the problem, but she can't reach him and fears he'll be late again. If he were around more, none of this would have happened. Joyce thinks longingly of her special brownies, stashed in the drawer beside her bed. She tries phoning Blondie, but her friend doesn't pick up.

Now, Joyce calls Jessica into the kitchen, steeling herself for confrontation.

Her daughter claims some other girl snapped the picture with Jessica's phone. "I only sent it to Chloe. I swear we didn't mean to hurt anyone. We just thought it was funny."

The phone lies between them on the island, straddling the stain, sequins and glitter scattered like cinnamon. "I'm sure, sweetheart. But how did the rest of the class get it?"

Jessica shrugs and blames automation. "That's why they call it a sharing app, Mother. Duh."

Joyce stares at the image, Liza's child shivering, exposed. Is this how Liza felt years ago? Slinging beers and cheeseburgers, boobs trembling, a Maddie seed already planted in her.

Seeds. Where did they get those seeds?

Jess denies that she and Chloe are growing anything more potent than lima beans. "I swear, Mom. Cross my heart and hope to die." Her finger traces an X across her chest. Then she folds her arms and aims her chin at her mother. "Anyway, who are you to talk?"

Joyce can't have heard right. She reaches for her ear, as if she needs to adjust her Bluetooth. "What? What did you say?"

"Oh Mother. Everyone knows about your brownies."

Everyone?

"I told Chloe it would be sooo funny if you put those out for the teachers."

For an instant, Joyce panics. Then she remembers that only the store-bought brownies made it onto her china platter.

"That is not amusing, young lady." She hears Mrs. Farnsworth saying those exact words thirty years ago when she confiscated Joyce's paper fortune teller.

Jessica snickers.

"That's it. No cell phone for you for the rest of the month."

This time, her daughter isn't laughing. Both of them grab for the phone at once. It slips away and crashes to the floor. "If anything's broken it's your fault," screams Jess.

Joyce stares in disbelief. How can her child have so little empathy?

The cat, who's been lurking in the doorway, chooses this moment to slip between them. He lays a paw on the phone, just the way he plays with his toy mouse, shoots it across the room and tears after it.

Jessica glares at her mother. "I should post a picture of your stupid brownies."

Joyce claps her palms over her ears, but she can't stop looking at this stranger, her daughter. Jessica strides to the end of the room, picks up the cat, and drops him on the counter where she knows he's not allowed. He licks at the stain. The two of them, Jess and the cat, stare back at Joyce. The cat's eyes are yellow slits, fortune tellers blinking *open | shut | open | shut*. Jessica's eyes are stony gray, unforgiving as granite.

Barns Are Painted Red Because of Dying Stars

by Heather June Gibbons

Paint splatters the farmer's overalls. He steps back
to admire the barn, a fresh coat glistening in the gory
sunset, a few bruised clouds against an orange sky,
and wipes his brow with a red handkerchief.
Red, a compound of oxygen and iron, elements
created by the nuclear fusion of stellar explosions.
Red, the first color babies can see. At dusk, his wife
comes out, careful not to slam the screen door,
and stands with him before endless rows of soybeans.
The first star appears, then another, all of them dying
or dead. Some just cool, expand, and collapse.
The biggest ones bloom into supernovas, blasting
chemical reactions into space, seeding the universe.

Birdwatching

by Claire Chafee

My older brother Ted had a tendency to wear his hair un-combed, in this one certain way. Strangers had to crush the impulse to lean across and flip a piece back across his head. He looked like he had been hung upside down and quickly turned back upright, unexpectedly.

Never without a field guide, trying to spot rare species in New York City, he went on secret expeditions to Jamaica Plains to watch the birds at 6 a.m., packing binoculars, keeping lists. Was he watching them or was he hunting them? The growing suspicion that you should not want to see birds that badly.

In and of itself, it doesn't sound that crazy. Nothing in and of itself does. But if you've ever been in the company of an obsessive paranoid, you know the sound of the coin inside you when it drops and churns, the way they used to do in buses.

My brother also had what a trained psychiatrist would later call "a shoe obsession." Again, in and of itself, not that bad. Plenty have one. Walk-in closets full of options. But he insisted that his toes were bumping up against the inside leather. His shoes were keeping him from things: from listening, from staying in the eighth grade, from knowing who he was. His shoes were against him. I can picture desert boots, eight pair in boxes stacked beside him at the StrideRight. The salesman with his metal sizer. Nothing fit.

He killed a songbird once. Shot it through with a bow and arrow. He had been aiming at the birds all morning with his finger guard meticulously strapped to his hand. It was summer and the scream that came, the scream in the middle of an afternoon of humidity, was buckling.

I was on the roof of the studio, bongo-drumming on the drainpipe to the Beatles, singing "For I Have Got, Another Girl." I climbed my secret way down and ran to see him crashed through a plate glass window or lying like the letter K against the ground, but instead there is this bird, still moving in tiny efforts, its staring eyes un-closable.

My father was the one to pull the length of the arrow out. My mother seemed more upset than she was equipped to be. We weren't up to this, any of us. But it was what we had been expecting.

Later that year, my mother was driving on the Merritt Parkway. I was in the passenger seat and Ted was in the back. I was in a pair of corduroy pants the shade of marigold. I was twelve, Ted was thirteen. I did not know how things would get so enormous or I would have checked the threat level. I would have used my Doppler radar. The language of weather prediction: how calm and dire at the same time. High wind advisory, possible flash flooding. Those are things I should have seen that day, as he was flipping the little metal ashtray on the armrest in the back—flicking it open and closed, open and closed.

But instead, this is what I see:

My brother's hand on the back of my head, pushing my head forward from the backseat. My forehead hitting the windshield. My front door opening and my mother pulling the car over. Me running down a gravel incline like I've seen them do in Hitchcock movies. The scene is in black and white. Me thinking, me knowing, I can prove this, now there's blood. I play this out. I watch it happen.

I am almost a goner. I am running as fast as I do in dreams, and he is right behind me.

Eventually he stops and so do I. I am very far from the family car. My mother is halfway outside the car, her hand still on the wheel. She is screaming something I cannot hear. I am seeing the aerial view.

I am bending over, out of breath, hands loose on my knees, slippery with blood. I'm looking straight at him. I pause. Wait for the cops to come? Wait for the next step? Never not known the next step. I do not move a muscle. If I start to run, so will he. I somehow know this is my fault. Running makes them chase you; it's the instinct kicking in. Other cars have noticed us now. I have made evident the unspoken and I am going to pay for it, letting the violence spill out like that, but that is worth it, even the need to throw my clothes away when I get home. That is worth the highway gravel stuck in my hands. Travel is in me now.

Genetically Modified Breakfast

by Diane Fiedler

Good Fortune

by Marley Stuart

—*for Christine Schmidt*

There is perhaps no joy as great as this:
sliding spiced peach strudel still hot from its tray
to a white paper box for the woman
at the register who came in asking
for something with peaches, her daughter's
face pressed to the case and warped golden
by the lights like a face in a dream.
They walk out laughing at their good fortune,
holding the box between them, leaving
only a few crumbs, fragrant steam.

Patron

by Marley Stuart

He buys a brownie
and a miniature pie, sits
with his back to me and eats.
There's something of my friend
in him, the one who just died,
and I wish I knew what it was.
The black T shirt, ripped and flecked
with paint? The jeans with drywall
compound dried on the knees?
Whatever it is, he wants nothing
to do with me. He flips down white
sunglasses and crumples his paper
tray, leaves without a word.

Later, he tells a friend
at the job site, laying tile,
Don't go to the bakery
down there by the bank.
The stuff's all right.
But the guy just stands around
and stares while you eat.

Political Machines

by Alex Ahmed

*I*recently caught up with the teaching assistant for an undergraduate humanities course I took years ago, that helped inspire my subsequent studies. I told him that everything I thought I knew about academia was wrong. He wryly responded, "Did you, too, think it was about the pursuit and advancement of human knowledge?" Now that I'm a PhD student myself (the position my TA was in ten years ago), it's clear to me that going into academia isn't necessarily any more pure or noble than working for a corporation. They are intimately intertwined, and have more in common than they don't: trying to bust unions[1], fueling gentrification in surrounding communities[2], and contributing to global warming[3]. These realizations haven't disrupted my academic work, but they have gone hand-in-hand with my taking a more critical stance towards my field of research.

I'm studying health informatics, which is about building technologies that aim to support health needs. It sounds like a good thing, right? But since I started my program in 2014, my previously unchecked enthusiasm for how technology could benefit the world has been thoroughly checked. What concerns me are not the usual anxieties about lifestyle (social media is causing us to forget how to have friends!). Rather, I've become alarmed at how tech hubris–the conviction among tech people that we're a disruptive force improving the world–makes us blind to the ways we're a conservative element, reinforcing structural inequalities. Technology is not neutral. It is not apolitical, and we must grapple with that.

Tech Isn't Neutral

One of the most often discussed ways that tech isn't neutral is algorithmic bias[4]. Turkish, my mother's language, uses a gender-neutral pronoun. But Google Translate injects these sentences with sexist stereotypes.

The same thing happens when translating other languages that use gender-neutral pronouns, such as Indonesian and Finnish. So for Google Translate, it seems that men are doctors, women are nurses, and she can only love him. When Mashable asked Google to comment, a spokesperson stated that they are "actively researching" how to deal with these "unsolved problems in computer science." But their response obscures the unsolved political problem underpinning the technical ones.

Assuming that Google cannot feasibly alter the biased data that feed its algorithms, the company has the responsibility to design a solution. They could, for example, make use of the fact that English already has a widely accepted gender-neutral pronoun[5]. And yet, singular "they" is still mocked as an example of "political correctness," thus delegitimizing non-binary gender identities. Rather than perpetuating misogyny through its translations, the software could take an active role in normalizing the use of singular "they," or at the very least providing it as an option within the interface. Although the company may be concerned with taking a political stance, its apolitical public response is actually a stance in favor of the status quo.

Other consequences of algorithmic bias are more directly and deeply harmful. A "risk assessment" algorithm called COMPAS predicts the degree to which a convicted individual is likely to re-offend (also known as "recidivism")[6]. Judges across the country use this output to determine prison sentences. A recent analysis by ProPublica indicated that COMPAS was "particularly likely to flag black defendants as future criminals, labeling them as such at almost twice the rate as white defendants[7]. In addition, white defendants were labeled as low risk more often than black defendants." The labels themselves were also uninformative: people who were flagged as likely to commit a violent crime actually did so only 20 percent of the time.

This practice reflects the inherent institutional racism within the United States prison system[8]. Believing in the algorithm's supposed impartiality allows all political and ethical responsibility to evaporate: the Supreme Court refused to hear the case of a Wisconsin man, Eric Loomis, who was given an 11-year sentence without probation for attempting to flee an officer and operating a vehicle without the owner's consent. Meanwhile, the COMPAS algorithm remains closed-source and proprietary; it cannot be seen or modified by anyone outside the company, which refuses even to disclose how it works. (The code and methods ProPublica used to conduct its analysis are available online.[9])

In another technical area, speech recognition software often fails to recognize accented voices, often because the datasets used to train the algorithm don't include them[10]. Conversely, white, educated, first-language English speakers tend to be most represented. Researchers noted that the underrepresented groups in these datasets tend to be groups that are marginalized in general. The consequences of these flaws of design and implementation are carried forward in our society — as a direct result, these underrepresented groups are going to have a harder time using the technology (and finding it useful).

But the story doesn't end there. People sometimes perform false accents, or use a "machine voice," in order for voice-responsive technologies to correctly understand them.[11] This issue can be viewed through the lenses of colonialism, assimilation, and white supremacy. The failure of the technology to recognize and act on the voices of some individuals mirrors the failure of our society to provide equal access to resources based on race and nationality. Framing this issue as purely one of missing data forecloses on a structural analysis of the ways technologies are embedded in sociopolitical contexts. Rather than just incorporating data from marginalized people (a reformist solution based on notions of "diversity" and "inclusion"), we might also attend to our methods of software development and design. In what ways are they inherently oppressive? How might they be changed?

Anti-Political Machines

Meryl Alper did extensive research on Proloquo2Go, an app used to assist people who cannot produce oral speech[12]. On the surface, it is difficult to see why this app could ever be problematic—its function is relatively straightforward, and it aims to address a human need. Alper found that more privileged families were able to benefit the most from the tech. Privileged families are better able to navigate educational institutions and obtain the required training to use the software. Importantly, media narratives tend to uplift the technology and its creators as the salvation to people who, due to their disability, are somehow deficient.

This provider-recipient relationship is not merely an invention of the media. It's constructed by the technology design process itself, which privileges the decisions, actions, and abilities of the designer. When first mapping out research projects, it is not always the case that the recipient populations are consulted. It's even rarer for a member of that population is a decision-maker on the design team. This is not an accident: this is part and parcel of a system that reinforces social inequalities, while innocently proclaiming an intention of social good.

We can find some context by taking a brief look into the history of "tech for social good." Lilly Irani wrote that "the rhetoric and practice of development positions emerging nations as essentially powerless and unable to 'develop' without intervention."[13] In this way, the field of developing information technologies for "developing countries" maintains a power relation in which the recipient of the technology is powerless without it. This relationship is identical to the one enacted in the design of assistive technology. In these cases, oppressive power relations—colonialism and ableism, respectively—aren't just unfortunate side-effects of technological development. They are symbiotic. They cannot exist in their current forms without each other.

We've known this for a long time. In his article "The Anti-Politics Machine," James Ferguson argues that when technical systems are uplifted and promised as solutions to poverty, they mask political reasons for why people are disadvantaged in the first place[14]. This works to the advantage of those in power, because it creates "uneven relations of economic dependency" between US-based industries and people whose lives have been historically—and are presently—impacted by colonialist violence. With this lens, we can begin to see that tech saviorism and white saviorism are two sides of the same coin.

Despite these glaring problems, many researchers in technical fields have taken up a mission to do "social good." And they often do it while being completely separated from social justice work—or worse, from a position of political "neutrality." However, as Joyojeet Pal argued, these are serious problems that deserve to be considered in their entirety, rather than in a way that is most convenient or self-serving for the researcher[15]. This necessitates a direct engagement in politics. Depoliticizing research is harmful not only to the people whom that work directly affects, but also to our research processes itself.

Following the work of Sara Ahmed and many others, we must recognize that "all forms of power, inequality, and domination are systematic rather than individual."[16] In other words, the biases, beliefs, and intentions of individual software developers do not fully capture the extent of racism in the tech industry. While some developers may indeed be racist, this limited view prevents us from examining the systems in place that ensure racism is never challenged (such as a company's hiring practices, leadership structures, policies, and priorities). Ahmed puts it clearly that "eliminating the racist individual would preserve the racism of the institution in part by creating an illusion that we are eliminating racism." This means that simply including more "diverse" people on a development team is not enough to combat oppression. In other words, it's not just about getting into the room. It's also about what we're able to do and say while inside, whether we're listened to—and how long it takes before we get pushed out.

Science for whom?

Human-computer interaction (HCI) researchers have argued that egalitarian approaches to the design and implementation of technology result in a design environment uniquely rich in relevant information.. As Nunes writes: "it is a great challenge to know what 'needs' to be designed... A strength of the HCI lens is its ability to embrace this complexity, for example, through the use of qualitative methods."[17] In contrast to quantitative methods, which are primarily concerned with the measurement of variables and the statistical relationships between them, qualitative research uses in-depth interviews (among other tools) to develop a holistic understanding of a topic. In the field of software development, participatory design prioritizes the needs and values of users over the specifications of designers.

But it is not enough to base our science on recruiting "diverse" participants and calling it done. The Ejército Zapatista de Liberación Nacional (the revolutionary indigenous resistance movement, also known as the Zapatistas) recently organized a conference called "Las ConCiencias"[18]. There, scientists and activists came from around the world to explore the transformative potential of an anti-capitalist science wielded by and for indigenous communities. Zapatista Subcomandante Galeano asked profound questions: "With all of the damage that the capitalists have done to the people through their misuse of science, scientifically can you create a science that is truly human in order to avoid falling into a science that is inhuman? And if it is possible [to] create a truly human science, who can create it?"

These questions remain open, but opening them was itself important. In my work, I want to ask what transformational opportunities might look like in health informatics. Despite lofty social goals for developing "technology for health," the field has been (rightfully) the subject of criticism. Take some of our favorite buzzwords, which are often held up uncritically as admirable: "open" systems, "disruptive" technologies, "innovative" approaches. These terms imply that anything that helps you to bypass institutions is, by default, empowering or liberating. But is this the same as equality and justice? For example, calorie-counting and exercise apps often ignore how our social and political situations are deeply intertwined with our health outcomes.

The goal for my dissertation is to build technology for transgender health. In order to do this, I have researched[19] how our medical institutions have historically pathologized trans people and perpetuate oppressions that continue to this day[20]. I've also used qualitative methods to look at the feelings and experiences of trans people as they relate to technology and identity[21]. It's impossible to do this work responsibly without engaging in political questions, especially because the word "transgender," and our existences themselves, are politically loaded.

Long before news broke that CDC researchers were cautioned[22]against using the word "transgender," I was advised that my chances of receiving a fellowship from a major government research institute would be hurt if I used it in my application. Currently, I am trying to find funding to continue my research while also contending with discriminatory and anti-worker practices in the university[23]; these conditions are among the major motivating drives for graduate employee unionization[24]. Although my immediate future is uncertain, I am sure that my development as a scientist and as an activist are connected. And I want to keep learning how to be better as both.

Endnotes:

[1]http://www.truth-out.org/news/item/40530-penn-state-university-wages-union-busting-campaign-against-its-own-graduate-students

[2]https://www.huntnewsnu.com/2017/03/as-northeastern-population-grows-so-does-impact-on-neighborhoods/

[3]https://www.theguardian.com/news/2017/nov/08/us-universities-offshore-funds-endowments-fossil-fuels-paradise-papers

[4] Check out Safiya Umoja Noble's new book Algorithms of Oppressionfor more on this topic.

[5]https://qz.com/923238/even-the-staunchest-grammarians-are-now-accepting-the-singular-gender-neutral-they/

[6]https://epic.org/algorithmic-transparency/crim-justice/

[7]https://www.propublica.org/article/how-we-analyzed-the-compas-recidivism-algorithm

[8]https://www.nytimes.com/2017/10/26/opinion/algorithm-compas-sentencing-bias.html

[9]https://github.com/propublica/compas-analysis

[10]https://www.wired.com/2017/03/voice-is-the-next-big-platform-unless-you-have-an-accent/

[11]https://www.theguardian.com/technology/2016/feb/10/texas-regional-accent-siri-apple-voice-recognition-technology

[12]https://merylalper.com/giving-voice/

[13] Irani, L., Vertesi, J., Dourish, P., Philip, K., & Grinter, R. E. (2010). Postcolonial Computing: A Lens on Design and Development. Proceedings of the 28th International Conference on Human Factors in Computing Systems – CHI '10, 1311.

[14] Ferguson, J., & Lohmann, L. (1994). The Anti-Politics Machine: "Development" and Bureaucratic Power in Lesotho. The Ecologist.

[15] Pal, J. (2017). CHI4Good or Good4CHI. Proceedings of the 2017 CHI Conference Extended Abstracts on Human Factors in Computing Systems – CHI EA '17, 709–721.

[16] Ahmed, S. (2012). On being included: Racism and diversity in institutional life. Duke University Press, pp. 44

[17] Nunes, F., Verdezoto, N., Fitzpatrick, G., Kyng, M., Grönvall, E., & Storni, C. (2015). Self-Care Technologies in HCI: Trends, Tensions, and Opportunities. ACM Transactions on Computer-Human Interaction, 22(6).

[18]https://freerads.org/2017/04/04/zapatistas-reimagine-science-as-tool-of-resistance/

[19]https://www.researchgate.net/publication/318571065_Transgender_Health_Disparities_A_Technosocial_Epidemiological_Approach

[20] Giffort, D. M., & Underman, K. (2016). The relationship between medical education and trans health disparities: a call to research. Sociology Compass, 10(11), 999–1013.

[21]https://www.researchgate.net/publication/321276094_Trans_Competent_Interaction_Design_A_Qualitative_Study_on_Voice_Identity_and_Technology

[22]https://www.washingtonpost.com/national/health-science/cdc-gets-list-of-forbidden-words-fetus-transgender-diversity/2017/12/15/f503837a-e1cf-11e7-89e8-edec16379010_story.html?utm_term=.d59edb82282e

[23]http://www.alicolleenneff.com/blog/2017/11/8/on-academic-precarity

[24]https://thebaffler.com/the-poverty-of-theory/laboring-academia

Window Guests

by Maximilian Heinegg

1.
Near summer, the sparrows my wife calls
affectionately *dirt birds* nested behind our AC—
we woke at five to their shrill colloquy.
My neighbor emailed if I thought it wise,
& more loath to offend than to disturb,
I unscrewed the plastic accordion edge
& floated the light braids of twig & leaf
to the herb garden, but after, I found
a powdery blue egg on the nursery ledge,
& having overstepped, left it there.

That evening, we drove our brood to range
beneath the strawberry moon
the Algonquin named for the berries' peak,
the only one we'll see for seventy years.
Unimpressed, the girls scampered down
Robbins Farm Park's hill as we picked it,
admiring *pink pink pink* about our final
rose moon risen & we, its fading guests.

2.
Teachers on the hill in June & Boston marked
the moon in its clear field, the talk of last bells,
summer schemes & students floating away,
our years atomized out of relevance
to the fugitives from our tempered dens,

classroom windows clear again.

On the longest night of the year
the science teacher found Mars, Jupiter, & Saturn
with ease, its rings seen as a single gold star,
& told me that as I'd touched the egg,
the parents would never warm to it again.

A bad student myself, I feigned facility, turning
back to the straw beneath the berry,
the city's graphite, the moon
sharpened for me as a kindness.

In July, the dirt birds returned with their stark
alarm set for dawn. We let them stay.

Lab Mouse Litany

by Angelo Mao

Black eye beginning to pale
from the center, turning white
delicately towards the edge of fur.

Black eye beginning to pale
for the law of air descends
and dries the glisten of meat.

Black eye beginning to pale
in the stiffening body, in its socket.
The black eye as pale as tendon.

Black eye beginning to pale
in a feint. This one, anesthetized,
had forgotten to blink.

Black eye beginning to pale.
Bodies curl around stiff faces
behind the freezer's marble door.

Black eye beginning to pale.
A bird has no qualms shrieking.
What did it learn last night?

Black eye beginning to pale.
The sternum snipped and pulled
back and taut, a paper fan.

Black eye beginning to pale,
a heart beating in the dead thing,
and other wonders of the world.

Black eye beginning to pale
in the freezer of wonders. Exiting
with empty hands again.

Black eye beginning to pale.
Opening the ribs. Heart. Lung.
Spleen. Twin kidneys. More fat.

Black eye beginning to pale.
Is there any red like the thick red
of the spleen, iron and soft?

Black eye beginning to pale.
There is no shape like the liver,
neither leaves nor a cupped hand.

Black eye beginning to pale.
But a blood-drained liver would look
like a continent, and as thin.

Black eye beginning to pale
in this deconstructed body.
Spread, catalogued, informative.

Black eye beginning to pale.
My gloved hands are lubricated
by this oiled thing called life.

Black eye beginning to pale.
Doors slide open and close easily.
My haunches move me easily.

Black eye beginning to pale.
It will be bioengineered eyes
that stare back from the future.

Black eye beginning to pale.
So sings Orpheus's severed head,
but instead of singing I open.

Black eye beginning to pale
for the law of air descends.
Ribs spread out like a paper fan.

Halogen lights are shining outside.
A heart beating in the dead thing.
Black eye beginning to pale.

The Asshole

by Vincent Yu

*H*e was not a very good person. He was, by many accounts, vile, impolite, crude, inappropriate, ignorant, insensitive, and offensive. He was a gifted asshole, a precocious prick, a well-rounded, ahead-of-the-curve, 40-under-40 douchebag--the kind of person whom other people enjoyed coming up with names for. He was a blacklit dickstain, a snarling cockmonster, an ingrown hair that fucked a hangnail and birthed twin abscesses of the mouth.

His name was Bertrand. He lived on the eighth floor of a building uptown whose elevator had been broken for as long as anyone could remember and would likely remain that way, seeing as he was its superintendent -- a job he despised. He liked to say that a superintendent was basically a glorified handyman, which was not surprising -- in part because it kind of *was*, and also because he was the kind of reductive, belittling person who liked to say everything was a glorified version of something else.

His refusal on most days to address cracked toilet bowls and clogged sinks and a rat problem that was gradually moving up successive floors must have accounted for great swaths of free time during which he developed the alcohol tolerance of two full people and the weight equivalent of three. Complaints lodged against him were scattered like ash over the ocean -- his old man owned the building, after all, and several more like it across the city, and before the housing market crash had been quite rich.

On the days he endeavored to go outside, after the thunderous descent of his haunches had shaken the building like mortar rounds and scandalized several families who mistook his traveling grunts of exertion for an act which he, in his persistent virginity, had never experienced, he would visit the subway. None of us knew where he went or what he did, though we resented him all the same.

Most of us had lost our jobs after the big market armageddon. Those of us who were saved the indignity of unemployment checks were dangling by split hairs from temp gigs at gasping companies whose FTE staff had been hacked to hollow bone. The majority of us had degrees from four-year colleges. Greg on the fourth floor was even a philosophy PhD, though few of us sympathized and even fewer agreed to call him "doctor."

He was known to reduce people to their most unpleasant features -- there was Janet, the loud walker on the third floor whose footsteps were like a hiccuping earthquake; Helena, the failed actress whose smile was 80 percent gums; Brandy, the pink-haired performance artist who was about to lose the Cold War standoff against her parents and move back into her childhood home in suburban Virginia; and Desmond, the sassy gay accountant who was way too sassy to actually hold a position as tame and boring as that of an accountant.

He was a man of few words and many grunts -- he snorted up silver-dollar-sized loogies and hocked them over his piss stream, into the urinal. He drank water from plastic gallon jugs of Poland Springs. His fridge purportedly contained nothing but an array of squeezable condiments -- goopy bottles of ketchup and off-tasting mayo, grainy tubes of dijon mustard whose dispensation bore a disturbing resemblance to the passing of kidney stones.

His body was like a bar of used prison soap melting in the sun, like a muddy, early-spring snowman without the middle thorax. He was a prodigious hoarder of calories who did not need to iron his shirts because the extension of his paunch kept every article creaseless. He put up notices riddled with misplaced apostrophes *"Please do not loiter in the hallway's past midnight."*

His favorite beer was Miller Lite.

The music began suddenly on a morning in August. A pleasant series of major scales and arpeggios repeating faster and faster. Some jazzy improvisations. Single notes held for many minutes at a time.

"Trumpet," said Marta, who lived on the third floor and had graduated from conservatory. "I can tell that he's had some formal training. He's got a great tone."

Some of us rolled our eyes at her.

Others made friendly visits to the fifth floor to introduce ourselves, bearing individually-wrapped sleeves of hydrox cookies, asking non-invasively into profession, family, job connections, freelance opportunities, schooling, and reported back to the rest of us.

"Does he go to music school?"

"No."

"Does he play in an orchestra or a group?"

"No."

"So he just busks on the subway for money? That's his whole life?"

"Yeah."

And we all nodded thoughtfully and smiled at each other -- *what a wholesome, bohemian thing to do* -- and when we ran into him we apologized on behalf of the shitty superintendent of the building, who was a real asshole.

We invited him to our vegetarian-friendly dinner parties and offered him hits of our weed and plastic cups sloshing over with red wine. We added him on Facebook and LinkedIn and Twitter and promised to query our friends about any low-key gigs that might arise. We were surprised and a little bit dismayed to learn that he'd read nearly every book already discussed in our reading club. We asked him how he'd come up with 12 months of rent upfront and he smiled and shook his head, as if that were enough of an answer.

We told him about Sharon, who lived on the fourth floor and whose January rent was once a day late and how Bertrand, in apparent retaliation, had cut off her heating for a week, during which time she caught a cold, lost her voice, and missed an audition for a role on a sitcom pilot which was later picked up and nominated for an Emmy.

"I knew the casting director, too!" she'd cried into our arms. We all agreed that Bertrand really was an asshole of hemorrhoidal proportions.

We told him how Bertrand never even took out the fucking trash. How the garbage chutes were so hideously backlogged that everyone from the fifth floor down was forced to pack their refuse tighter and tighter into a solid wall of filth, like some kind of reverse-jenga. And how Susan, the comedienne on the second floor, once saw him mix the recycling and trash into the same receptacle.

We warned of his tendency to put glue in our keyholes if we were late for rent, and how he'd once made a leering pass at Samantha from the third floor, and when she rebuffed him, flipped the circuit breaker in her room. We casually alluded to the rumor that he refused to let Asian people move in, and how he'd once been spotted throwing a kitten out of a second floor window.

The building itself was a dirty, slummy hovel. Mosaic flowers dotting the floor were worn and chipped, the railings induced splinters, and the few windows which dotted every other stair landing looked into a perpetually dark alleyway in which certain homeless men would tie up or avoid the police or both.

Our neighborhood was just the wrong side of authentic. We were flanked by check cashing storefronts whose lines snaked around the edge of the block, liquor stores run by Asians who'd installed thick, plasticky walls to glass in the merchandise, dusty bodegas that were not charming, random 3 a.m. detonations that we could only hope were cars backfiring. There was a Crown Fried Chicken down the street whose dark, grainy oil was at least a week old at any given moment.

We felt particular resentment towards our living situation on those nights when we attended parties in high-ceilinged erstwhile warehouses in trendier parts of town, where the brick was added to look exposed and the HVAC snaking across the ceiling was shinier than IKEA displays, where we talked about l'Objet d'Art and snorted occasional lines of coke and grumbled at how -- of course -- whoever lived here probably had rich lawyer parents.

We announced with no little pride how we'd deleted our dating apps because it was all just *too much*. We chased cooler versions of ourselves, we bled out our savings, we had a communal stash of condoms, we took digital photos of Polaroids and used them as profile pictures. We were the least materialistic group of people in the world -- we valued *experience* over *things*. We strove to make good puns on the internet, to straddle the line between relatable and remarkable. We lost hope slowly, in tiny flecks that gradually wore away, until our ambitions wobbled atop rusty trestles.

We leaned left, but not too far. We despised the collective evil of European imperialism, toxic masculinity, unacknowledged white privilege, the 0.1%. We rolled our eyes in the direction of finance or consulting types, but acknowledged that those whom we knew personally seemed like decent enough people.

We protested, mobilized online, called our representatives, donated to charities, angrily failed to understand conservative principles. We gathered ourselves when our parents came to visit. We shrugged off their vaguely horrified looks and insisted that the state of things was perfectly fine, that -- no, thank you -- we didn't need any help, that we had no interest in moving back home, that we agreed -- yes -- the economy would rebound, that we'd start getting more realistic, that we'd consider grad school.

We had panic attacks when we reached the age our parents were when they had us.

Most of us had moved to the city because that was what you did in those first early years, living hard and fast, having no-strings sex, edging your credit limits, burning the candle at both ends, accumulating enough experience to tide you over through your dismal, sagging thirties.

We dreamed but dared not hope that we'd get our big breaks early -- that we'd make the 30 under 30 lists, that we'd make enough money to never have to ride the fucking subway again, that we'd return triumphantly to our class reunions with awards and achievements.

But Sharon, who'd graduated at the top of her acting class, still couldn't win any roles past off-off Broadway, and of those, none that didn't involve partial or full nudity. And Tim, the visual artist from the third floor whose style had once been compared to Basquiat, had so thoroughly burned through his fellowship money that he was reduced to selling caricatures to tourists on Fifth Avenue. Ned, the ambitious and self-proclaimed novelist amongst us, had yet to place his work anywhere outside his college literary magazine.

Shana, who was a dancer, had partnered with a young composer on an experimental project filmed in an abandoned warehouses that married the sounds of the modern metropolis with the jagged, hypnotic movements of its mindless populace. All of us had agreed that the idea was amazing, that nothing like that had ever been done before, and that it had the potential to be deeply impactful in certain artistic circles. The ensuing video had peaked at 1,000 views.

Some of us got jobs as line cooks and busboys and waiters.

We hosted open mic nights in underground, tucked-away theater spaces and silently declared ourselves funnier, more artistic, more authentic, more compelling than the people who performed. We had working screenplays for crazy, stranger-than-fiction, genuinely hilarious one-person shows about our experiences growing up.

The more practical among us wanted jobs as editors at Norton or FSG or valuators at Christie's or Sotheby's or musical directors of the Metropolitan Opera. Others wanted to be paid to travel and be creative. All of us wanted to capture things about our lives that others missed, and to get into high profile arguments online.

We downloaded productivity apps and sent blizzards of resumes into the deep freeze tundra of the job market. We enjoyed the sounds of the trumpet player practicing. How the notes that seeped through our single-ply ceilings were buttery and soft, like marbles rolling in paint and streaming across the floor.

We bemoaned how much *stuff* was being made -- all the pre-packaged, microwavable, quick-fix bites of entertainment that satisfied the masses. We hated how many people there were crowding the streets, standing on the left side of the escalator, blocking the intersections without proper right of way, sticking their hairy, sweaty arms into the elevator just as the doors were about to close and then riding it up to the third fucking floor. All those people not paying attention to *our work*.

It was all we could do, some days, not to take our collective rage out on the singular Bertrand, who was everything bad about people distilled into one horrible person.

Instead we took deep breaths and went to hot yoga. We told ourselves over and over, *at least we weren't Bertrand. At least we weren't him.*

Bertrand possessed the kind of learned helplessness that made him averse to exercise because his knees were worn down and was incapable of diet because of thyroid issues. He was able to obsess so persistently over whether or not he had anxiety that he developed actual anxiety, like spinning shit out of thin air, and fairly soon had a bulk stash of Xanax

He was an arrogant cynic, the kind who thought his pessimism was a sign of superior intelligence. He harbored a distrust for *corporations* and *government.* He possessed the kind of doublethink capacity to despise unfair labor practices but purchase cheap clothing on sale.

He liked to use the word *sheeple* unironically. His bookshelf was purportedly a sticky window ledge on which a soft, crumpled paperback edition of *Walden* lay stolen from the library. He had an honest and difficult time understanding why people found Thoreau insufferable. He had a gut feeling that he was destined for something more. And which feeling, growing with his gut, became unwieldy and fairly tragic and extremely hilarious.

He hassled delivery people with imaginary grievances, demanded free food until he was gradually blacklisted from every Chinese, pizza, and jerk chicken place within a half mile of the building. He was spotted tripping a toddler, throwing rocks at a stray dog, and once, making as if to drop a quarter in a street junkie's cup before taking it back and *eating it whole.* He once spilled the contents of the building's septic tank across the front entrance to prevent an HUD rep from entering.

Cyndi, who'd frequently referred to Sharon as a bitch in college but had reincarnated as her friend and roommate, claimed to have found evidence of Bertrand's online presence on an internet forum, on which he defended the Republican president and called someone a "complete idiot" for supporting Medicare.

The group of us who gathered in their apartment to investigate found no doxxable evidence but nonetheless enjoyed mocking the contributors on the *Intelligent Conservative* forum, especially the person who was probably Bertrand.

Tim and Jenna on the third floor were trying to land TV gigs by coming up with unoriginal yet slightly offensive sketch comedy routines. Jenna, for her part, was Hispanic on her mother's side, so she was safe from problematic issues. Their belief in going viral -- in that one hilarious video that would get picked up by the *Huffington Post* and transmitted through *Buzzfeed* -- was impressively austere and reminded us of the red-haired Buddhist who'd lived on the second floor landing, meditating all day in bare feet, until Bertrand lifted him by his arms and threw him onto the street.

Tim and Jenna were perhaps a couple but probably not, because they didn't want to be hassled by romance and potential jealousy if their joint thing took off. So they limited sex to those evenings or afternoons when they got too drunk or too high and remained publicly ambiguous in order to drive up potential gossip.

Eventually they moved to pranks. He videotaped himself putting ketchup packets beneath the toilet seat, giggling. She videotaped herself tossing pitchers of ice water into the shower when he was in it, staring into the camera and stifling her laughs as he shrieked. The views poured in a bit more steadily. They upped the intensity. She waited behind a corner for him to walk in before slapping him in the face with a raw salmon fillet. He stole her tampons and replaced the interiors with standard Kleenex.

When they reached 50,000 subscribers, a small talent agency contacted them about possible representation, which they happily accepted, and celebrated with a multi-floor party that was, of course, shut down by a waddling Bertrand at 11 p.m.

"This party -- THIS PARTY IS OVER!" he shouted, framed against the open doorway. We hadn't even heard him knocking. Jenna drunkenly offered him a drink.

"No, no, guys, come on!" He reminded us giggingly of a student teacher in over his head. "Come on! Is that *weed* I smell?"

Across the room, someone slid open a window and stooped out.

"Hey! That's for emergencies only! Get off there! Get back in there!" Bertrand yelled.

Pink-haired Brandy, high as fuck on whatever was in the cloudy pipe being passed around, started wobbling atop the third-floor landing, shouting, "Fuck you! Fuck you!" from the other side of the window.

"There are families in this building, too! There are sleeping children and old people. You *NEED* TO KEEP IT DOWN!!"

"You're a fucking asshole. You don't do *anything*. You just hang around harassing people and living off whatever the fuck this bullshit building is worth."

A sharp chill was pouring in the through window. We wondered, shivering, why Brandy had decided to move outside in order to commence her argument. We wondered, too, how she could not be freezing her ass off in the fishnets and leotard. Someone whispered "performance," and half of us seemed to understand a bit better.

Erika from the fourth floor was a multimedia artist who was neck deep in a sex-positive video project where she explored the masculinity of various Asian men firsthand. Most of us found this kind of off-putting, although we preferred her to her roommate, Ava, who had dreams of blogging her travels around the world and in the meantime, openly shoplifted from the Sephora she worked at, spending all her non-working hours testing different kinds of eyeshadow and liquid mascara in front of her computer camera, scraping for YouTube views.

On a cloudy, humid day in April, the two of them adopted a baby schnauzer named Marty from the local animal shelter, much to everyone's delight. He was energetic and friendly and curious, and most of us could confidently say that his arrival was our most positive life development of the past six months. We definitely preferred him to his human parents.

We loved hearing his little paws scampering up and down the stairs, scratching at various doors until someone opened up and fed him something. We gathered more frequently on the landings between floors, passing Marty between us, smoking furtive joints and joking with each other.

Even the trumpet player ceased practicing in order to join us.

But apparently, having a pet was in direct violation of Rule #3B of the Tenant Agreement that Bertrand had tacked to all our doors and forced us to sign under penalty of no electricity. When that asshole found out about Marty, he called animal control, which arrived in the form of a timid man who gave Erika and Ava the choice of on-the-spot euthanasia for whimpering little Marty or a trip back to the shelter, where he stood at least a snowflake's chance of being re-adopted.

And as the caged van drove away -- as we all stood there sobbing and comforting each other and plotting ways to kill Bertrand without leaving a trace -- we heard a little dirge coming from the window of the trumpet player's room. Taps, played long and slow and solemnly, as they took away our best friend.

The trumpet player continued to fascinate us. He was lanky but not underfed. His hair was a perfectly rounded afro. He wore shirts with anime characters and knock-off aviator sunglasses indoors. Gerta, on the fifth floor, claimed to have slept with him and gave him a decent score.

"How'd you find this place?" We asked him.

"Just stumbled on it."

"How'd you get so good at trumpet?" Marta asked.

"Well I just practiced a lot. Didn't have much else to do growing up. And then my Pops gave me his old trumpet, and it just felt right."

"And, uh, what about your pops?" Ned asked, even though some of us nudged him because we found the implications of his question impolite.

"Dead," the Trumpet Player said.

"We're so sorry."

He shrugged. "Didn't draw up his will properly. When he died the government got everything. I had to hide the trumpet so they didn't take it. Eventually figured out busking made more than minimum wage, and the subway was at least a roof over my head."

We gasped. "You lived in the subway?"

The Trumpet Player nodded. "Not as bad as you think. Cardboard becomes soft after a while. No one really bothers you when it's late."

We were awash with pity -- the unfathomable, saw-it-on-the news kind that welled up in us when we read about things like mudslides in Sumatra and civil wars in Africa. We were, for a moment, collectively transfixed at how cruel life could be and how unfeeling the world was and how undeserving this poor Trumpet Player was of all the shit he had to deal with.

"But how did you get the money to live here?" Ned asked.

"It's complicated, but some people helped me out, and I saved up."

We appreciated his stoicism and his quiet dedication to his art and we wished him the best of luck, thankful that none of *us* happened to be brass players, too.

On the morning the music stopped, Bertrand was showing a room to a potential tenant.

"I'm not sure we have availability yet, but maybe you'd like to take a look?" Ned heard him saying in between wheezes up the stairs.

"And then he asked her on a date!"

We were shocked into giggles.

"She was completely out of his league."

"Any woman would be out of his league."

And for days we made jokes about how absurd it was that Bertrand would ever harbor the idea of attracting another woman, not to mention *this* woman, whom most of us hadn't seen, but whom Ned described as 30 at most, a wavy-haired brunette who wore Keds with a sundress and carried one of those *New Yorker* tote bags you got with a year's subscription.

"And get this," Ned said. "He asked her to grab coffee and she said she didn't know when she was free but she gave him her number!"

"Damn, you can't say he doesn't have guts," Marta said.

"Is it really him having guts? Or is he just completely fucking insane?"

We snickered at his attempts to clean himself up. How cinching his pants at the waist seemed to cut off blood flow to both hemispheres of his body. How his sweat-stained wife beater was clearly visible beneath an overstretched button-up. We noticed him walking down the subway stairs again and wondered how this might be connected to all the recent developments.

And then, on a hot afternoon, Bertrand asked us for advice.

"I'm not too -- too great with this kind of thing," he said to a group of us hanging out in the lobby.

"Not too good at what?" Marta asked innocently.

"I know you all know. This lady. I'm not good at this stuff."

There was a tremendously awkward pause.

"Well," Ned began. "Well, women like it if you show interest but not too much, you know? Hook 'em in and then just back off. I personally like to compare them to famous women in literature, you know, Helen of Troy or Dante's Beatrice or, you know, if she's really up on her knowledge, Petrarch's Laura."

We rolled our eyes at this, because Ned was a borderline sexist and self-averred snob and none of us had ever seen a woman entering or leaving his room who was not his mother.

"But don't play games. No one wants a person who's just playing games," Marta said.

"But don't be too forward, either. It's creepy."

At this, most of us burst out laughing, even as Bertrand sat emotionlessly, taking however many mental notes would fit in his Post-it-sized brain.

"Compliment her eyes." "Keep things casual." "Read women authors." "Don't tell immature jokes." "But still be funny." "Never let yourself do all the talking." "That's right, ask questions." "But you still have to be interesting." "But don't try so hard." "And don't come off as too eager." "Yeah, wait a day to call back." "A day? Fuck that. Wait a week." "I waited a week once and he took it for disinterest and moved on to another girl." "It was a 'he'?" "Sweetie, I hate to tell you this..."

"Definitely go for coffee first," Marta said. "Coffee is just informal enough for there to be no pressure, but still possibly a thing."

We admitted to ourselves that he was beginning to look at least semi-human. There was a lightness to his wrinkles, a softness of his skin once the gritty layer of stubble was scrubbed off.

He was humble and pathetic in the way that adoration could make you.

Then in private, we approached Tim and Jenna, who had reached 78,000 subscribers and were in talks to star in a web-series and were getting pretty fucking smug about it, and asked for prank advice.

"Put peanut butter in his shampoo container," Tim said.

But none of us had access to his room.

"Change the shortcuts on his phone so that when he types certain words they turn into swears or something," Jenna suggested.

None of us had access to his phone.

"Jenna, don't you work at a coffee shop?" Brandy asked.

Jenna stiffened. "I *used to*. This new deal is gonna bring in enough money that I don't need to work there anymore."

"But you still know people who work there, right?"

She nodded.

The plan emerged smoothly after that. Bertrand would take the young woman to the coffeeshop where Kate worked but was about to quit from. Behind the counter, we'd spike his drink and film the conversation and its aftermath, which Tim and Jenna would post on their YouTube channel.

Their date fell on a Saturday in July. We'd done our best to make Bertrand look acceptable. Ned lent him a razor attachment that left a fashionable amount of stubble. Dmitri lent him a skinny tie from J. Crew. Ava gave him quick haircut and applied some sort of a gel that she'd stolen from Urban Outfitters.

"Make sure to eat a big breakfast beforehand," Ned told him. "Otherwise the caffeine will overwhelm your system and you won't be able to stop shaking."

We waited about three minutes after he left before passing

quickly down an adjacent street, passing through an alley and reaching the back entrance of the shop, where Jenna let us through.

"Wow, she really is pretty," Brandy said, as we hid behind the shop's counter, gathering at Jenna's knees.

"Is he there already?"

"This might be the most he's ever walked in his life. His ankles might give out."

"Shut up, he's coming up, he's coming up."

He ordered a plain black coffee, she a cappuccino. Jenna smiled and said she'd bring the drinks over to their table. The small vial that Ned tipped into Bertrand's cup, before Jenna handed it back, read "'ipecac."

Those of us below the counter listened closely. Jenna's camera was zoomed in and focused on the two of them at a table at the far end of the room, next to a wide window that faced the street. The front door had an old hinge that gave a distinct squeak every time it was opened, followed by the metallic jingle of a strip of bells. The hot fizz of the espresso machine punctuated a low murmur of conversation.

"What are they talking about?"

"I can't hear shit."

"This is the bougie-est coffeehouse playlist I've ever fucking heard."

"Wait. wait- "

"Oh SHIT!"

A sick, splattering sound. We stood up. Bertrand was still vomiting. It had splashed over the table -- a chunky, sour smelling mess -- and landed on her blouse and dripped into her *New Yorker* bag.

"Jesus! What's wrong with you?" she shouted.

It spilled across the floor and nipped at the shoes of disgusted fellow customers.

"Ugh! Ugh!" she retched. "This is! -- You're! -- Get away! Get away!"

"I don't know what's -- going --" a final grapeshot of puke hit her face before she stood up and tore out the door, leaving a friend-ly tinkling in her wake.

A beat of silence. Then Bertrand stood up and stared at us, be-hind the counter. Pure, putrid terror on his face. Jenna's phone was still recording.

"I'll, I'll pay for all this," he mumbled. "I'm sorry."

He drew a hairy arm across his mouth (we'd told him to roll up his sleeves; women loved forearms) and pushed out his chair and stepped out. The familiar creak, then jingle of the door.

Jenna pressed the stop button. The murmur in the shop began again, but reconstituted. It became pointed and angry. They were all shuffling out the door. A manager came out from the back, look-ing horrified.

"Guys, that was awesome. This is gonna go viral," Jenna said.

"This, that, wasn't as funny as I thought it would be," Ned said.

"I mean, he deserved it, right?" Marta asked.

"He was an asshole, and he's made our lives hell for the past few years. Of course he deserved it," Brandy said.

"Who's cleaning this up? Who did this?" The manager was a slim, middle-aged man. "Jenna, why were you recording? Who are these people?" as he gestured to us.

She shrugged.

"Well you have to clean this up! Whatever happened, you need to clean it up now!"

"Well, actually -- actually this is *perfect*."

Jenna handed her phone to Ned. "Can you record this, please? Pan over the room before you get to me."

Ned did as he was told. Jenna saw him out of the corner of her eye, noting his sweep, seeing him land on her before shouting,

"I quit! Suck it! You can clean this all up yourself, ASSHOLE!"

She skipped out, careful to avoid the vomit puddles. The rest of us followed, a little meekly.

The awkwardness subsisted after a few blocks, as we approached the apartment building.

"I wish the trumpet kid were there. He would've appreciated that," Ned said, buoyantly.

"Bertrand probably kicked him out though -- probably thought he was too noisy or wasn't paying enough in rent," said Dmitri.

"He looked so young. He probably didn't even threaten to sue."

"Oh, did you guys not know?" Jenna said suddenly. We shook our heads.

"Bertrand was letting him stay a few months for free."

"What? Why?"

She shrugged. "Ugh, it feels so good to be free! I fucking *hated* that job."

"To be honest, I don't really feel like going home yet," Brandy said. Some of us agreed. There was a cheap bar nearby, someone said, two or three stops on the G line. A smaller group of us descended and took the train in silence.

When we reached our stop, as we battled the inconsiderate assholes trying to stream their way in when some of us were still trying to get out, we heard something familiar. The same, marbling tone. The same ribbony jazz.

It was our Trumpet Player, standing in the middle of the platform, his cheeks blown out like a squirrel's, his eyes closed and his whole body slowly gyrating. A black case sat open by his feet, in which sat a handful of crumpled dollar bills and glinting coins.

And sitting right across from him was Bertrand. The collar of his shirt was completely soaked through. Small islands of puke stains dotted his body. He was sitting back with his legs out and listening.

Walking along the City's Nerve

by Cory Hutchinson-Reuss

she makes of herself an ache   a succession of waves
foaming   a corridor of ginkgos that flash in the storm

She moves among others   trespasses the contour of the public
where certain bodies can't wander without question

When she says it's *very dangerous to live even one day*
she means the day   contains multitudes   despite the lie

at every empire's core   a story that claims the right of way
Is it bravado   or is it a stranger, interior witness

when she gestures toward the cityscape to name it
as her own being   certain   that she & the stacked apartment

balconies   crosswalk signs   rows of saplings & the wasp
with its elegant legs   radiate from a shared locus

a numinous ventricle she tries to recall with every encounter
Still the sky coalesces into one chalky color

People pause to watch a cloud of passerines roll & flux
They might be siblings   or magnetized shards

She patterns a prayer of shoes & illuminated faces
Glass store fronts hold a body of birds   brief

span of tremor & patina that reminds her of a friend's
heart   bursting a wide road   a tremolo of stars

It syncopates her walk against a nation's vast
web of pavements   the crush & stricture of its parade

She notes the wobbly cup the fibrillations   every blood-
hint on the sidewalk where people now spill

forward   their faces candied in red light   in blue flashes
of emergency   the word a vehicle for *arise, to bring to light*

To expose the cargo as the state of things

Note: "Very dangerous to live even one day" is from Virginia Woolf's Mrs. Dalloway

A Butterfly Story

by Mike Sinert

The room is the color of Andes chocolate mints, the kind I once ate by the handful from a crystal bowl on my grandmother's coffee table, and a mess of folding chairs holds a dozen heavy women chatting, a few silent guys, average sized, and a handful of thin girls, too thin, skin the same faded green as the walls. Meeting in Progress, reads a sign on the door. It's handwritten, yet anonymous.

I've got a hundred pounds on everyone here. One-twenty-five. I feel fat and out-of-place, more ogre than man, less macho than hungry.

There's a Biker Dude twirling a pack of Marlboros. Or Winstons. I can't tell. The red logo's blurred.

I want one. I don't smoke. Never have.

A girl with scraggly black hair stands, quieting the room, and my eyes go straight to her chest. Not to the obvious, but to the tattoo centered between the exposed straps of her bra. A butterfly, large and swirly and blue. I stare. For too long. Until the chant starts. I've heard it before. Dozens of times. On television. In movies. It's bullshit. Nonsense for the alcoholics.

God, grant me the serenity to accept the things I cannot change, the courage to change the things I can, and the wisdom to know the difference.

Oh god, grant me some fucking fried chicken.

And the Butterfly Tattoo Girl says, My name is Marni and I am a compulsive eater, and everyone says, Hi Marni. Everyone but me.

I'm fixed on her ink. I'm not a tattoo guy. Never was. But this one has me. The detail, the style, the intricacy. The sharp contrast with her rotted teeth. She's a puker. Stomach acids eat the enamel.

Not me, thank heavens.

And she says, I am sitting with these open containers of take-out around my kitchen table. It's barbecue. I'm saying to myself I'm only going to have a few bites. Just a little. And then I have a bite, and another. And I'm saying no but soon I'm eating right from the containers, with my hands and my fingers, and then I'm filthy and sticky and soon it's all gone and I run to the toilet and make myself vomit and then I want more and I hate myself. Again.

She's crying, and something hits me and suddenly I want to cry. I don't, but one day not long from now,

when my belly is stuffed,

when I'm fighting the urge to vomit and clinging with despair to the fullness pressing from the inside out,

when a therapist asks why I binge and I won't open my mouth for fear of losing it all,

I will cry.

It's like when I masturbate, the Butterfly Tattoo Girl says. Sometimes it's too much and I want to stop but I can't. So I keep going. Over and over and over. I keep eating and purging and eating and I can't stop. It's my escape. It's how I don't feel.

Whack job.

But she's not. I know what she means. Not about the purging but the desire, the hideous craving I feel every moment of every day,

and will for another decade-and-a-half of secret, compulsive eating,

for another eighty, ninety, hundred pounds.

We're more alike than I can admit, eating to escape, to hide, struggling with our crazy, searching for structure, any kind of structure, to keep us from the depths of our addiction.

One day I'll know.

Right now she has more guts than me, this blighted, filthy person, standing before a roomful of strangers, exposed to the world, sharing her worst. All I can do is gawk at her chest. At the butterfly. And she asks, Will that next binge make you happy? Will it fill that void? Food's not love. Learn to love yourself. That is the path.

My path is burgers,

pizzas,

Chinese.

I want a hit, I need it bad, and even her retched-up barbecue sounds lovely. So who's the whack job?

Control your compulsive eating or it controls you, she says. Control it or they control you–

the salt and sugar-suppressed feelings you can't bear to feel,

the chemical engineers, with their umami-inspired, hyper-processed, neuron-warping, highly addictive delights, feeding

the corporate-controlled supply lines — pre-packaged, convenience stored, super-sized, Kentucky Fried, Golden-Arched, plumping

Wall Street profits and shareholder values, at the expense of waistlines and self-esteem.

Control it all or it all controls you, the Butterfly Tattoo Girl insists. Work the plan. Trust the higher power. It's one day, one meal at a time.

Higher power. That's it. That's what she's got, despite her teeth, her hair.

It's that tattoo.

And for a fleeting moment, I imagine her butterfly is mine, drawn beneath the dark hair of my own chest, blackened into the skin above my own beating heart. My redeemer. My salvation. My satiation.

But it is not to be. I am not a tattoo guy. Never was.

I stand and turn for the door, acknowledging what I already know. What I've known all along.

The Biker Dude whispers, Stay, man. We'll talk after. He holds out a smoke. A Winston. I push past and run, a hard move for a man carrying so much. My mind already steps ahead.

Reality: I've been planning the binge since the girl with the tattoo first uttered the word.

Barbecue.

I have no control. No plan. No higher power.

No butterfly.

Moon Raises a Glass

by Lynn Holmgren

Imagine Moon, incognito, at a downtown bar.
Shades on, collar high, maybe even a brunette wig
While we're at it. She's not there

To make small talk. It's winter and the shifts
Get long. She becomes thirsty — gazing
Out over air strips, deserts, cornfields, jungles —

Imagine, having such a strange and disparate brood
To call your own, to watch over every night while they hustle
And bend the dark to their will, or sleep, stalks bent.

In the bar she becomes the space between
The smooth, dark wood and the drinks
That drift across it to fill in for what's missing:

A Cookie Made of Sugar, Butter, and Family Memories

by Jennifer Packard

S andbakkels are thin Scandinavian sugar cookies made from pale yellow dough pressed into fluted metal tins. They emerge as buttery creations in the shapes of stars and flowers. Every bite of this crunchy-on-the-outside, soft-on-the-inside cookie brings me close to family members, even those who are no longer with me.

The first bite: While I look on, my grandmother and her sisters bake a massive batch of sandbakkels. They gossip and laugh while they work. My grandmother tells a story about her neighbor's car that broke down the day after it was purchased. My Great Aunt Ardis talks of an old boyfriend. She switches to Swedish for part of the story deemed too adult for my young ears. When she finishes, the women explode in laughter. Their hands seem to work of their own accord as they magically press the dough with their thumbs while spinning the tins.

My grandmother gives me a tin and a bit of dough. For ten minutes, I try to perfect a single misshapen sandbakkel. Despite my sad looking cookie, my grandmother and great aunts encourage me. "That's good," they tell me, "you just need to press the dough thinner."

The second bite: As my grandmother ages, my mother takes charge of the food preparation for our family gatherings. Together, she and I listen to music while we make the sandbakkels. Our words flow easily as we focus our attention on pressing our dough into the tins. Together, we eat up any cookies that fall apart when they are removed from the tins. These cookies are deemed to be "testers." I ask my mother how my cookies look. "They're good," she tells me, "you just need to press the dough thinner."

The third bite: I am both excited and nervous as I move away from home to my first apartment. I open a carefully-wrapped housewarming gift from my Aunt Jan. My eyes tear up when I see the set of sandbakkel tins. "Whenever you need it, sandbakkels will give you a taste of home," she says. "Just remember to press your dough thinner."

The fourth bite: My grandmother and her sisters are gone. My mother and my aunt live half a country away. They whisper to me as I make sandbakkels with my own children. My grandmother tells me she's proud of me while Aunt Jan reminds me that I am strong. My mother encourages me to keep going. These women who were my first teachers guide my hands as I press the dough with my thumbs while spinning the tin with my fingers.

The kitchen grows warm as the sweet aroma of the baking cookies fills the air. My children and I carefully pop a batch of finished cookies out of the hot tins. We laugh together as we compete to be the first to taste the broken pieces. As we start the next batch, my youngest son proudly holds up a tin full of dough and asks me, "How's this mom?"

"That's good," I tell him, "just press the dough thinner."

Sandbakkel Recipe
1 cup sugar
1 cup butter, softened
1 egg
1 teaspoon vanilla
1 teaspoon salt
2 ½ cups flour

Cream together the sugar, butter, egg, vanilla, and salt until it is well mixed and smooth. Add the flour ½ cup at a time until the dough is still moist, but not wet. Place a small ball of dough into the tin. Use your thumbs to press the dough onto the tin until it forms a layer that covers the whole tin. The dough should be thin, but without any holes or bare spots. Scrape any excess dough off the edge of the tin. Place the tins onto a baking sheet and bake at 350 degrees for 8-10 minutes. The cookies may be slightly brown on the edges. Remove the cookies from the oven and let them cool for a minute before removing them from the tin. They should pop right out of the tins, but if they don't, try gently squeezing or hitting the bottom of the tin until the cookies come out. Be careful though – those tins can be hot!

Our Lies Are Our Fondest Hopes—And Science Will Destroy Them (That's a Good Thing!)
by Benoît Rey

*I*never liked science. Numbers are boring. I never was this nerd guy, doing the math, imagining algorithms, checking things in a laboratory...I studied science only because I was told: you have to do something with your life. I am a good boy, so I tried. Hard studies. Bad memories. I became a scientific journalist, and started writing about physics and astrophysics. A good job: I could spend my days earning money without looking at the clock every ten minutes.

And soon I discovered science's secret and fabulous power: the power of pure destruction! Destruction of the magic, of all the myths we are swimming in, all the stories we have been told for centuries about health, about other human cultures, about the influence of the moon...Science destroys reactionary thinking. Politicians' lies. Science is a huge and cold machine that kills fascism. It destroys fake news piece by piece, as they were just a bunch of Amazonian trees. Science is Hiroshima on simplistic beliefs. It is Nagasaki on traditions, Fukushima on the status quo. It always questions why the world works the way it does. Why things are what they are.

I remember two years ago, after the terrorist attack at the Bataclan theater in Paris, French Prime Minister Manuel Valls said he was tired of people always looking for excuses or cultural explanations for what happens, and that to understand terrorists is to excuse them. And all the social scientists were like, « whaaat ? Did he just say that?» Yes, he did. This guy is a total asshole, it is a fact. And science will play a role in shutting up his smelly mouth.

Why are things the way they are, that is the question. By asking it you realize that everything happens for a reason, and hence that things could be different, that another world is possible. Science shows that the evolution of a system can be different if you change the initial conditions. So why not change _the_ system? Why not change society? We, the people, could use science for ourselves, like a guillotine that we wheel out, to remind the rich to shake in their boots. They have media conglomerates to attack our brains with lies. We can take science and destroy them.

Science is a weapon of mass destruction against stupidity, against oversimplification. Sorry man, but the alignment of the planets doesn't have anything to do with your life. It has been proven false one thousand million times. On the other hand, climate change likely played a role in causing the Syrian catastrophe, and hence also the terror attacks you may soon undergo... So tell Donald Trump that climate change has a lot to do with national security. (Good luck with that.)

Science shows that things are often more complicated than they seem. And that our intuition is often wrong. And that you cannot trust your sensations. Your brain is full of cognitive biases, it is always trying to cheat you, to save some energy, because this is its purpose. And maybe that's what makes us racists! If you are white, and you see a black person attacking somebody in the street, it's lazy to think damn ! how violent are the black people ! But how many black people are NOT attacking anyone in the same moment? And how many white people are? It might hurt your brain to think about it. Good.

If you want to get a glimpse of something closer to reality, you don't have a choice, you have to forget what you believe, what you see around you, and start considering the statistics. Science shows you the causes of events, the effects of decisions, at both the individual and global scale. Science reveals the hidden links between things. It awakens you to the filters between your pupil and your brain. It clears your vision of the world around you. It destroys the huge walls of this cardboard theater built around us, and reveals what is behind the scene. It is the perfect weapon to struggle against what *they* want us to believe, against what we deeply want to believe ourselves. Science killed God! In human history, that is quite something, isn't it? From the science point of view, God is no more than some simplistic concept adopted by cavemen. Man can see, so God sees it all. Man can know, so God knows it all. Man can create, God creates it all. After all, God is just the human being projected to infinite perfection. It is by definition what will always be unreachable. God is just an asymptote. God is overrated.

For all that I like science, and its corollary materialism, it kills our pretensions of having souls. We are no big deal. We are all manipulated by our chromosomes, our history, and after all, our free will is quite ridiculous. We are just big flabby bags of molecules. There is nothing to be proud of, and nothing to be ashamed of. Our feelings, memories, desires, dreams, all that constitutes our one and only cherished life is just the organization of a bunch of cells. And maybe that is where the problem starts. Why we fear the ideology science plunges us towards. Like a lot of scientists I know, I am always defending science when I argue with people. But even though it can be a fantastic tool for our emancipation, it still worries me. Because science has not much more to bring than that. It killed God, ok, but didn't replace it with anything.

After years of facing science, I am contaminated by its nihilism, and it won't go away. That's OK, I can accept that nothing is important. But meaninglessness is not that easy to live with. And I am not sure it can bring everyone on board. Indeed, it is not very sexy. Unless you have kind of a twisted sense of humor, it is not much fun to consider that you are only a flabby bag of molecules, that there were plenty of humans before you, and there might be even more after. You are just a try, just a tiny link of a huge chain that goes nowhere. So why struggle? There is no intrinsic meaning to existence. Don't take the ones already proposed, religions, politics… they have all proven wrong. They've all expired, and smell bad like a rotten yogurt. If you want a reason to exist, you will have to invent one. But be sure that science will destroy it, as it has destroyed all the others. This fantastic destruction machine is out of control. Accept that, and try to be happy, or don't. Who cares.

Icarus, in Old Age

by Vera Kroms

My feathers, to begin with,
were never fine -- just barnyard
leavings or the debris my father plucked
from village fields. He was desperate
to save me, to inflict me
with correctives -- restraint,
submission -- but I already knew
I was designed
for never dying.

There was a moment when I'd climbed
the air as high as possible,
when I sensed that this is what
a calling feels like, a severing
of every ligature
your world has spun you.

Oh, I plunged.
They got that part right.
Unwinged as I was born.

Flight is just an old
attachment now. And sun
the harshest witness.   I've been pasturing
in twilight, submitting to the thumb
of the eventual. No one's child,
with wintered hair,
cracking like an old painting.

Hitting the Wall

by Lâle Davidson

The first time Cassandra passed through the wall, she hadn't meant to. She had been standing at the edge of a retirement party at the hospital feeling as uncomfortable as usual, had leaned her back against the wall and fallen right through, finding herself in the kitchenette next door.

The wall was still intact, but a gritty residue of plaster coated her tongue. The sour flavor was almost pleasant, and her internal organs felt like they had had been scrubbed with a loofa sponge. If it hadn't been so wrong, it would have been right. She spit the residue into a wastebasket and re-entered the party. None of her co-workers had noticed she was gone.

She had always had boundary issues. The first time she heard the term was in her disastrous first marriage. "You're invading my boundaries," her husband had shouted one snowy evening, after they had been driving around screaming at each other for twenty minutes, and had ended up in a cemetery.

"Boundaries?" she said, looking out at the snow-covered tombstones hunched under the high beams. "What are those?"

That marriage ended as quickly as it began.

She connected to people instantly, feeling the bitter peel and raw substance of them, wanting to skip the small talk and get to the core—because time was passing like a speeding bullet about to burst life's membrane.

Nevertheless, as much as she connected to people, she felt a keen sense of separation as well. The phone rarely rang for her, nor did text messages ping. She felt there was something about her that most people found unlikeable, but she couldn't figure out what it was. She was intelligent and kind, as far as she knew, and people told her she was attractive.

Her second husband, a man fourteen years her senior, whose face was weathered from years of house-building and nude river bathing, tried to assure her that her dissatisfaction was only anxiety, that she was only projecting her own dis-ease. If it hadn't been for her second husband and their daughter, she would have been lonely. But together, the three of them lived in a bubble of paradise, feeding each other dinner with bare fingers.

Not surprisingly, neither her husband nor her daughter blinked that night when she shared the fact that she had fallen through the wall earlier that day.

From then on, Cassandra began to pass through walls on purpose. She'd press herself through her friends' and colleagues' walls like soft cheese through a grater, and then she'd coalesce on the other side. They never saw her because people only see what they expect. She, on the other hand, saw more than she expected, a myriad of details that people weren't sharing. Usually, it was something small, like the fact that Deirdre, her stocky office mate of five years, who masked her shortness by wearing three-inch heels that made her calf muscles bulge, sometimes picked her nose when Cassandra was out of the office; or that the director of marketing, known for her meticulous efficiency, had a leaky bladder and kept pads in the back of her desk drawer. Other times it was something momentous, like when Barbara, an admissions clerk, was quietly making burial arrangements for her husband, who had hanged himself. Yet every day Barbara had greeted her with the same exact set of pleasantries.

Each time Cassandra passed through a wall, it sifted her organs clean but clouded her feelings, not with what she discovered, but with the fact that so many people assiduously maintained such façades. She couldn't understand why.

"You might restrain yourself," her husband said with a smile at dinner one night, when she explained what she was doing. He wiped up the last of the hummus with a carrot stick and held it up to her mouth.

"But why?" she asked, letting him feed her.

He shrugged, scratching his white beard. "People like their privacy."

"But I've never bothered to cover my birthmark," she said, referring to the irregular wine-colored splotch on her left jawline. "If someone asked me how my day was, I'd tell them if it was crappy. Who is anyone kidding?"

"That's why we love you," her teenaged daughter, still in her bony stage, said as she plucked a Concord grape from Cassandra's plate and squeezed it until it burst its skin into her mouth.

After dinner, while watching TV, Cassandra braided and unbraided her daughter's hair, and her daughter, in turn, braided her husband's long hair, and then outlined Cassandra's wine-colored birthmark with a blue ballpoint pen.

"It looks like a ruby-throated hummingbird now," her daughter said, holding up a hand mirror. Cassandra looked at it distractedly. It did, indeed, look like a hummingbird, with its long beak probing the line of her jaw, wings reared along her cheek. She smiled, not looking at the rest of her face, which she thought plain.

Sometimes, when she shared personal things with others, her

colleagues and friends called her brave. Cassandra rejected this assessment, except for the day the subject of abortion had come up in the cafeteria one lunch period. The most outspoken among them was loudly proclaiming it murder. She felt compelled to admit she'd had an abortion at the end of her first marriage, and that even though she'd grieved the choice—had developed a drinking habit because of it that she'd later cured—she knew that giving up that fetus (she used that word on purpose) had cleared the way to the perfect peace she now shared with her second husband and daughter. Sharing this information had cost her a few heartbeats and a red face, but she wanted the silent among them to know that decent people made difficult choices.

When she told Deirdre this story, Deirdre gasped, pulling her chin back into her neck so that it formed a temporary double chin, and said, "Oh, I'd never do that." Cassandra was caught off guard, so she didn't ask if she meant the abortion or the admission of it. For a few weeks after, when she passed people in the hall and made flickering eye-contact with them, her smiles came out like grimaces, as she wondered if they'd heard the gossip about her and judged her. Nevertheless, she believed in the power of truth, and she believed her sacrifice had been worth it. The truth was supposed to set you free, after all, wasn't it?

One day, coming back from the X-ray department, rather than opening her office door with her key, Cassandra pressed herself through the wall. Deirdre hunched over her desk and whispered vehemently into the phone. "Why don't you touch me anymore?" She had kicked off her pumps under her desk and had tucked her feet around the base of her chair, as if looking for a place to hide.

Cassandra stayed long enough to figure out that Deirdre was arguing with her husband, and then she pressed herself back out. She waited a few minutes before she put the key to the locked door. Deirdre, just hanging up the phone, turned to greet her brightly, her pumps now back on.

"How are you?" Cassandra asked.

"Fine," Deirdre said.

"How's the family?" Cassandra persisted.

After a fractional pause, Dierdre replied, "Jim just got us tickets to a Broadway show. Can't wait. How's your family?"

Cassandra leaned toward her for a second, ready to tell her what she had just seen, but the smooth expression on Deirdre's face bleached the intention out of her.

"Fine," Cassandra said, turning away and sitting down to her computer screen.

All these discoveries would have been fine if she had possessed verbal discretion. But one morning, her office mate answered her usual how-are-you with, "I'm a little tired today."

Cassandra, unthinking, asked, "Are things any better with your husband?"

Deirdre stiffened, her pupils constricted like a hermit crab pulling back into its shell, and then she averted her eyes and excused herself. Since that day, relations with Deirdre were strained.

Another time in the cafeteria, in a conversation about fitness with the director of marketing, Cassandra took the opportunity to slip in that she'd heard that Kegel exercises could help with incontinence. The director ended their conversation gracefully, claiming she had just remembered an appointment. Cassandra couldn't tell if it was true or not.

Over time, it seemed that most of the people she knew avoided eye contact with her and kept their conversations shorter than usual, but she might have been imagining it. At night the closed circuit of her family's love still lit the darkness surrounding her, but at work she grew more and more angry.

Why didn't they like her? She had so much to give. She was kind, compassionate and nonjudgmental. In defiance, she continued to press herself through walls, as if the more she did it, the more right it would be. But the weight of people's distrust and judgment, real or imagined, began to compact her.

Each time she pressed through a wall, it got harder to do, until finally one day, she pressed herself up against a wall and both her body and the wall remained solid. She drew back, ran her hand across its smooth surface, and tried again. No go.

After she stopped passing through walls, she found it easier to keep her thoughts to herself. Though her relationship with Deirdre never recovered, and the director of marketing still gave her only strained smiles, new friendships grew. But they grew like invasive weeds, easily plucked. The freedom this new kind of truth had brought her wasn't the kind she wanted. Maybe her husband was right, and it was only anxiety. Maybe she created the disconnection with her own internalized insecurity that others smelled on her like pheromones. Then again, maybe she saw a potential for something others rarely availed themselves of, and she was a diamond that would remain largely undiscovered.

She and her family continued their orbit in a tiny sun-filled universe, and the phone sometimes rang for her. Texts sometimes pinged. But there were still times at work when the late afternoon sun slanted through her office window like an orange lozenge, that she would hunger for the sour prick of plaster on her tongue as if it were the only food left on earth.

The World's Timed Perfectly

by Joseph Johnson

So I'm told beauty can only break open.
& it's true: Yellowstone: a series of explosions.
Breath: one last thing feeling
your body, a sun gone down some used-up alley.
So sit two chairs, rusting in a clearing.
Such insignificance reddening into terminus, such ad
infinitum we all fall into. There are no night skies
in music, nor tendon. But imagine
an entrance into boil-temp
landscape, its perfect water cycle,
its dense pinecones. Imagine being certified
precisely, in forest fire.

Lately, the news holds me awake. We're turning tires
over insects, other facts of existence.
I pick through quills & pocket a jawbone,
hoping for scorn, humming the last chapter
& wishing it end well: geyser, geraniums,
dark thorns through long seasons.
What sent the heaven from them?
Our loud red viscera. Some wisdom.
So slowly a caterpillar builds its chrysalis,
humidity fixed, little mineral facets—
a lifetime—a tight grip
cutting the solitary figure we slip from.
An opening, timing our bodies to the storm.

New Year

by Marjorie Thomsen

I'm too mellowed
and lonely without
boning and paring

so one bundle of knives
at a time to the professional-
grade grindstone. Worn carbon

now shiny steel
fresh from honing. I wield
a paper-wrapped batch,

de-sheet in the heat
of my small, hungry kingdom.
All palm lemons,

prepare for greens—
fried capers, warmed parsley,
olives.

I eavesdrop
on my act: blades
are blades

of ache: crisp, icy,
extravagant, cut cold
butter. Darkish January,

I blindly
remove the head
of a fish and forget I haven't been touched.

Open-air Market

by Marjorie Thomsen

There's dew on the brightness of fruits and
vegetables. A man photographs this scene,
sends it to a woman he knows in another
country where it's winter. It will remind
her of when he was traveling through one
of her years. He's certain the robust and
wet lettuces will make her smell earth's
fragrance, think of her body's place where
he entered her with joy in the daytime.
Edible blossoms! He'll describe the whimsy
of cooking with marigold and dandelion,
hoping to replace the sadness that's fallen
into some of her chutneys.

*

The baker imagines confluence of great riv-
ers, salty and sweet. He began making ma-
ple-bacon doughnuts to heighten his once
valiant sense of smell and taste, fearing they
were on the decline. He detects a certain
imbalance of thought and feeling in his life:
he knows to prune his lavender but where's
his fervor for its full, purple flourish? By
experimenting with the pairing of textures
and flavors—coconut masala, sea-salted
bourbon caramel, ginger mango—some-

thing may break free from the marrow of
his bones.

*

A woman considers all the babies who
don't have to worry about what to make
for dinner. She buys eggs for a variety of
dishes and reasons. Twine on the carton is
unexpected and she's grateful: hemp, bow,
surprise. She says goodbye to the farmer af-
ter taking a pickled beet sample—snippets
of proud, blood-red root vegetable. He told
her about mystery heirloom tomatoes and
their desirability. Leaving, she remembers
her favorite short story about a woman who
loved all the wrong, hard men then adds a
quarter cup of cold vodka to her piecrust.

Father's French Fries

by Dariel Suarez

As a child in Cuba I couldn't stop eating my father's French fries. Once I caught a glimpse of him in our small kitchen, skimmer in hand, eyes fixed on our oldest, greasiest saucepan, I knew better than to go outside and play. As soon as he retrieved the first batch of sizzling fries, I would sneak up behind him, hover surreptitiously over the plate on the counter, and snatch one of the top fries. I would repeat this maneuver three or four times, sometimes opening the refrigerator as a decoy. Eating fries before dinner ensured that, if my mother decided to give us all equal portions at the table, I would have eaten more fries than the rest of the family by the end of our meal.

On a couple of occasions, Dad caught me red-handed. He would make an unusual sound, similar to what he'd yell to shoo away an intruding pet, followed by a "hey!" Though his tone seemed playful, he'd make a gesture as if to swat me away like a fly. I would scurry toward the living room, only to take a peek moments later, waiting for an opportunity to pilfer again. With the passage of time, this ritual was replaced by a more memorable one:

my father leaving his fries on an otherwise empty plate for me to devour. This has been, by far, Dad's clearest sign of paternal love for his oldest son.

From their firm yet bendable texture, their soft, almost spongy interior, and their sparkling yellow surface—like tiny, delectable sun rays—my father's French fries are simply irresistible. They have always been my favorite food. There was no gradual process in my tasty obsession, no unforgettable experience that suddenly attracted me to them. I've always been in love with this food.

A couple of days before my tenth birthday, my mother inquired about what gift I wanted. "I want a full plate of Dad's French fries," I told her.

Had there been other options—expensive toys, a nice weekend trip, a brand new pair of tennis shoes—I might have asked for one of them. But this was Cuba, early nineties, right at the beginning of the Special Period. You were lucky to have a decent serving of food in front of you twice a day, hence a large enough plate of French fries could put the family out of potatoes for a week. I was lucky when my wish was granted. It ended up being the best gift I ever got while living in my native country.

My mother and my wife have repeatedly asked me what it is about my father's fries I can't resist. They are intrigued not only by my insatiable craving, but by the fact I don't sprinkle fries with salt prior to eating, a custom in the majority of Cuban households. Those outside my family who've come to know me throughout the years, when learning about my obsession with Dad's French fries, often make the assumption that it's probably not the way he makes them but the quality of the potatoes he chooses. Regardless of whether he used the dirty, nearly rotten potatoes allocated through the rationing booklets in Havana, or the ones my grandfather occasionally brought from the countryside, or the Idaho and red potatoes he procured from supermarkets and local vendors in Miami when we immigrated there, they all taste the same.

Truth is, I can't explain or pinpoint the heart of my obsession. I could claim it's a combination of things—the taste, the feel, the memories—but in the end I believe my fascination is inexplicable. And I prefer it that way. I see it as a kind of spell, a touch of culinary magic I dare not disturb in fear that it may ruin my delightful relationship with the fries. As hard as I've tried, I've been unable to replicate my father's success, yet I dare not ask him what his secret is. I mean, what if I ask and the magic goes away? What if Dad starts to overthink it? What if he loses his touch? What if I figure out the trick and lose interest? The thought of all this alone scares me. I just say, bring them on.

Today, a mountainous plate of Dad's fries still has the same effect on me. It's a hedonistic experience I refuse to give up. That's why, whenever I call my mother and tell her I'll be dropping by for dinner, I hear my dad holler in the background, "Tell him we're out of potatoes!"

The Drop Off

by Jennifer Martelli

That last hot day of fall, I watched my daughter finally turn
away and look through the fogged backseat window of my car
while two friends buckled in next to her told secrets,

one little wet mouth cupped to a tender ear.
My hands at ten-til-two, my eyes on each girl, reversed
in the rearview mirror, all of us quiet, I idled the car

near the school, at the dead end of Ida Road. Last night's lightning storm
flooded most of the street, sewers overflowed,
winds downed the maples, spilled their innards, and the wires: some snakes

just as dangerous dead. The car's leather seats were dark,
oxblood, and soaked in expelled heat from all of us.
It smelled of rubber and something

electric, corroded. My daughter breathed on the window to make
even more fog: drew things with her finger: hearts, stars, her name.

Crossing Nguyên Du Street
by Fred Marchant

Hà Nội

Advice we had was to just step right out,
    like wading

in a stream. Motorbikes—hundreds of them—
    would find

a way around us. We must not be hesitant,
    for that

would throw everyone off. So, trusting these
    our friends

here on the street named for the poet of *Kîêu*,
    we leaned

into the traffic as if it were only a light wind
    flowing round

our faces. At that instant I tried to imagine
    a world

completely merciful, and belonging to those
    few who,

as they passed smiling, looked as if they just
    might forgive us.

Through the Windshield, or Why I Did Not Run

by Erin Pushman

I heard that car before I saw it, heard the telltale screeching of tires as they rounded the corner fast—too fast. I was standing on an East Lansing sidewalk, five feet or so from the curb, where Grove Street dead-ended into Linden, forcing a sharp turn. Behind me a row of bushes lined the parking deck I'd just stepped out of. Beside me two trees and a park bench occupied a triangle of dormant grass. Between me and the street lay a wide curve of sidewalk and a not-yet-melted pile of crusty late March snow. I thought I was far enough from the street to avoid the oncoming car, so I did not run like I could have. I backed away a step or two, thinking I was fine, safe.

As the Audi came, I did not run, but I heard everything. I heard an electric hum I'd never noticed before humming, humming, humming, inside the parking deck; I heard small rustlings from the row of bushes lining the brick and glass wall behind me; I heard traffic passing down Grand River Avenue, where it met the campus of Michigan State University a few blocks away. I heard the Audi—the tread of its tires on the pavement, the engine under the hood.

When I saw the headlights, I was already fixed in the glare of their trajectory. Even then I did not move. I stood on the sidewalk, headlight beams illuminating the air in front of my body, and whispered something like, *Oh*.

Some of what I know is pieced together—fragments from memory, East Lansing police reports, press photos, and legal documents. After the headlights, I remember feeling the flash of impact, seeing—for a moment—through the windshield, then lying belly-down in the bushes, my lips pressed into black Michigan dirt, pain ringing my body like smoke.

Only a few blank seconds passed between impact and landing. I can't remember those seconds of freefall, but I know what has been said about them by heart. We collided, the Audi station wagon, its passengers, and I. The Audi hit a tree next. Uprooted, the tree and I sailed twenty-five feet through the air. The Audi skidded a sharp arc and slammed into the brick wall of the parking structure. Airborne, I followed a similar course. My head did not bang into two metal outcroppings on the wall; instead I soared up off the Audi's hood, bounced off the brick wall, and crashed into a stand of bushes that slowed my descent to the dirt.

After the Audi stopped, and the guys pushed away deployed airbags, opened car doors, and stepped out, I heard the driver say, *Oh shit. I killed her. I'm going to jail for the rest of my life.* Then, I tried to scream for help, but my mouth was full of dirt and twigs.

Throughout my twenties, as I recovered from that accident, I wondered what the crash looked like from inside the Audi. Did its passengers see a short girl in a red coat, face paling in the headlights, standing in one blink before the car, and in the next blink, shot off the hood like a body surfer? Did they see the brick wall, then the tree, then me, distinctly? Or did everything blur? And if they did see me, what did they see me doing out there? Taking one or two footsteps backward, standing still, blinking? Did the sight of me scare them? Was there time to register a face or fingers or hair, time to see nail polish, a ponytail wound into a bun, lipstick?

But the guys in the Audi could not have been thinking of me. They would have been fixed on their own fates and the wall hurling toward them. Still, for years I went on imagining their perspective as if that vantage point could reveal something I couldn't figure out, pay attention to the girl I was that night, or at least explain why that girl stood still.

In the dirt, I am fully conscious. I know this. Dirt fills my mouth; it grits on my teeth and coats my tongue. It tastes of gardens and blood. I feel the dirt under my fingers. I need to get up. Under my feet, I feel nothing, but I know I must be lying down, face down. I need to get up. I try. I try again. Then a feeling enters. Each time I try to make my body move, pain wreathes me, a crown, a robe. The feeling flows in and out of my skin, its source unimportant, the whole thing peripheral and penetrating. It circulates. It winds. It is a wire, a warm wire, winding. I lie with it; it holds me; we rock.

Then the need to rise, to move, writhes inside me again. Again, I try. I cannot get up, and this is how I know: I am not okay.

This knowing sings in my head; I can hear it in words I am not speaking. Then the imagined words collide with real voices, male voices, guys about my age.

Shit. Oh, shit. Jesus Christ. Fuck man. These words are a litany, a chant, rising from somewhere behind me. The voices are close, but not *near*, not within reach. I absorb the words into my own head, and they reverberate off one thought: *I am not okay.*

Then one of the guys, the driver he must be, speaks a sentence:

"Oh shit, I killed her. I'm going to jail for the rest of my life."

No, I want to say, no, no.... But the dirt is in my mouth.

"Fuck. We gotta get outa here." And this time, the voice comes with another sound, the slip, slip, slip sound of fast feet running away. I try to look toward the sounds. Nothing. The sound slips past my head and away down the street. They are gone.

"Jesus Christ. No, man." One is gone.

"Oh, shit, I gotta get outa here." Two voices left. I can hear the difference between them.

"No, man, it'll be worse if you run."

"I killed her. I gotta get outa here. Shit."

Two voices arguing, to stay, to go. I am hidden in whatever is all around me blotting out light. I am hidden, or they would see me and would know.

I spit out some dirt.

"Fuck, fuck," one guy says. My tongue is heavy. "Fuck. Let's get out of here." Same guy.

"I don't know, man." Different guy. I swallow. Dirt grits down my throat. In my mouth, the papery confusion of twigs and leaves.

"Oh shit, oh shit." First guy—leaving? I lick a twig from my lips.

"No," I say. My own voice scratched, quiet.

"Come on, man." The leaving guy again.

"No. No," I say. My voice rising.

"Let's get the fuck outa here."

"No. I'm not dead. You can't leave."

"Dump this shit out," they are saying to each other. "Dump it. Dump it." Then the sound of liquid hitting the ground, glass breaking.

"I need you to call 911," I say. I concentrate. I need to make sure I am saying these words out loud.

"Fuck, man. Fuck."

"Call 911," I say. "I need you to call 911."

The guys do not call. They do not run away. They do not answer me. Liquid hits the street. Glass breaks. I listen.

Other sounds are coming now, other students, my neighbors leaving their houses. Doors open, storm doors slam shut. Feet jump down porch steps, run down pavement.

"What's goin' on, man?" a new voice asks.

"Hey, what happened?" We are packed tight in the student ghetto. Students hear loud noises, react to them. It's around eleven p.m., early in student-time; everyone is awake, and people who heard the crash are coming outside.

"I need help." I'm shouting now. "I need someone to call 911." *I need I need I need I need...* these two words roll over each other inside my head. I spit them out as much as I can. "I need someone to call 911."

"I called. They're coming. Where are you?" Another new voice. A guy's voice too, but different. This voice is urgent and getting closer. And this voice is for me. "Where are you?"

"I'm down here." Am I crying?

"Where?"

"I don't know. Down here."

"I can't see you. Are you in the bushes?" The bushes. The voice orients me. The bushes along the parking structure's wall.

"Yes. Yes. I'm down here."

"Tell me what you need," he says. "Tell me what you need." *I need. I need. I need. I need.* "Hey?" *I need...* "Hey! Tell me what you need, okay? Just tell me what you need."

"I need... someone to get my roommates."

"Okay, where are they?" The address materializes whole in my mind like a globe.

"Four twenty-seven Grove Street, Dean, apartment three." I have to get everything right. "Kate and Lelaine."

"Okay," the voice says, "apartment four?"

"No, apartment three."

"Okay, Dean, apartment three. Go get her roommates." I hear more footsteps running down the street toward the Dean, which I know now, is behind me.

"What's your name?" He's close now, getting as close to me as he can.

"Erin." He gives me his name too. I can't hold the name, but maybe it's Scott, and now someone knows who I am, and he is saying he's going to stay here with me until help comes.

I've seen nothing since the windshield, have relied on sound to orient me. Now I try harder with my eyes. Still nothing. I feel with my fingers and find a mask of dirt. I wipe at the grit around my eyes.

Behind me, the sounds of more people coming. They are quiet; when one voice rises, others shush it. "Quiet, you guys." "Hey, be quiet; he's talking to her." They are listening to Scott and to me. I hear their bodies gather together, feet shifting on asphalt. Scott makes quiet rustling sounds, trying to move toward me through the bushes. Even the guys from the Audi have hushed themselves. It's so quiet I hear the guy Scott sent to my apartment. He must be there, at the front stoop, talking to my neighbors who are coming out.

"Apartment three. Where is apartment three? I need apartment three."

"Okay, okay," says a girl's voice. "It's down here."

We are all college students, these people gathering in the street tonight; we are typical Big Ten students—we know the fight song, we know how to tap a keg; we walk or bike to our classes, but we don't keep close tabs on each other. I've probably stood beside some of these people at house parties, sat a few rows away from them in lecture halls, walked past them on the sidewalk. But we are strangers. I do not know the students hovering around me. But tonight they come together like a trauma team, like they aren't college kids at all, but full-fledged adults. They're here, and they've called 911, and they're getting my roommates. I start to slip a little, down into my body. Pain like white electricity, coursing. I cannot see.

"Talk to me, Erin." Scott says. "What's going on?"

"Okay," I say. Tell it. If I tell Scott what is happening, I can keep going, and I have to keep going, at least until there is an ambulance.

But what is happening down in the white heat of my body has no lexicon; it does not exist in language.

"I'm just..." I say.

"Talk to me," Scott says.

"Just eating all this dirt," I say. Tell it, I think. "In my mouth. I'm breathing it. I'm trying to get it out of my eyes."

"Okay," Scott says. "That's good. Just...just keep doing that." The more dirt I clear from my face, the more I can feel and taste something else. It slips over my eyelids and between my lips, slides under my fingers. I tell this too; I tell it as it comes to me:

"There's something. There's wet on my face. Oh, God. My head's... bleeding; oh, God, I'm not okay." Around me, the students register my words. Breaths go up, the hush breaks.

"Her head's bleeding."

"God."

"Christ, that's bad."

"We need to—I don't know, that's bad, can somebody..."

"I don't know. We need some..."

"God, I don't know."

The other students and I set in to panicking now, and we're still the only adults here.

"Okay, okay," Scott says. "You are okay. You're going to be okay." And we all believe him; we all calm down.

Other feet come: Kate and Lelaine, their voices, beside Scott's, telling me they're beside me.

"We're right here, E." But I cannot see them.

Then sirens are whining toward us. An ambulance, please.

"The police are here," Scott says. Not an ambulance. But help is here, and the students in the street turn into kids again. No one is quiet; people start crying, start shouting about how bad the accident is, how bad I am. I join this regression, or lead it.

I am crying now.

"Calm down, calm down," an officer's voice says. "Everyone step back now. Everyone move back." Someone is crawling toward me, under the bushes. Branches snap—one of the officers, getting close.

He knows my name is Erin—Scott must have told him, or Kate or Lelaine—and he says it, "Erin," every time he talks to me.

"Erin," he says. "You are going to be all right, Erin. Erin, take my hand." Big, warm fingers rub over my knuckles.

"Take my hand, Erin."

And I do.

Back in October, in the Dean, apartment three, Kate, Lelaine, and I celebrated Halloween as an almost sacred holiday. We planned it for weeks, decorating our apartment and fashioning costumes from items we'd scrounged from the Salvation Army and our parents' attics.

We dressed as a party of dead prom queens, donning Goodwill tiaras and scavenged prom dresses from the '60s and '70s. We fashioned sashes out of wide ribbon and a permanent maker and draped them across each other's shoulders: *Prom Queen, 1966, 1969, 1973.* I wore my mother's dress, butter-yellow, grosgrain and dotted Swiss, empire-waisted, bell sleeved, trimmed with velvet ribbon.

1969: my mother's senior prom. My father came home from Michigan State University, rented a tuxedo, and bought her a corsage. In a photograph, they stand in Grandma Dorothy's living room, framed by the drapes hanging around the front window. Beautiful, they smile, my mother's hand wrapped around my father's arm. My mother's hair is long, long, parted in the middle, shining and straight.

When I unzipped the vintage dress and slid my body in, it fit me better than my own prom dress had, the yellow velvet ribbon cinching the fabric beneath my breasts. "That dress looks like it was made for you," Kate said, lowering the 1969 sash over my shoulder.

Dressed, we pinned dead corsages to our shoulders, painted our faces white, and drew dirt marks and blood onto our skin with muddy lipstick and dark eye pencil. We stuck leaves in our hair to make ourselves look like we'd just come up from the ground.

Months after my accident, my mother told me that as she and my father drove through the darkness on I-96 toward Sparrow Hospital, she didn't know if I would live or die. Without cell phones, my parents drove suspended in an hour of not knowing. My mother said she tried to imagine what she would dress my body in, for the funeral. None of my clothing seemed right.

This night was one blinking, sirened night in the midst of a Big-Ten college town where pedestrian versus motor vehicle was not a new story.

Three weeks before my accident, a group of three girls trying to cross Michigan Avenue late one night were struck by a drunk driver, but while I was still walking around, I did not pause to think about the incident. And not one week after I left the hospital, a package came from an East Lansing address I didn't recognize. When I opened the large envelope, I found a book of inspirational stories and a note.

Dear Erin, I know that you don't know me, but we share something in common. The handwriting was a woman's. *In the fall of 1995, I was also hit by a drunk driver while I was walking on the sidewalk at MSU...*

I'd been a freshman in the fall of 1995 but did not remember that accident. I must have seen news reports, heard people talking about it on campus. But the incident made no impression on me.

Then there was the story my father told me once, and never again. During his junior year at MSU, he was walking on a sidewalk near Erickson Hall. There was a crosswalk and a girl standing in it. When the car hit her, the impact knocked her out of her shoes. It was her shoes my father remembered most. "Her shoes were still standing there, man," he said.

That story had stayed with me, but only as a story, a macabre thriller, almost a fiction. I had never imagined myself walking, then, not walking. But wasn't that the same lack of imagination my mother had spoken of, not twenty years after she slipped the yellow prom dress over her head: *I knew it happened to women all the time, but I never imagined I'd have cancer...* Metastatic, left breast, left lung.

One police officer drew a sketch of the impact: a stroke to mark the beginning of the sidewalk, a line-drawn Audi, and a stick figure me. Who was the girl on that page—the one who thought she was safe on her own sidewalk, in her own shoes?

Only now, nearly twenty years after my first trauma, after sitting through the deaths of both my father and father-in-law, after caring for my mother as if she were a child, after sustaining a marriage for eleven years and counting, after birthing two children and miscarrying three more, after—daily—measuring our lives against the risks of what could happen: careening cars, exploding guns, childhood cancers, clowns in the woods, terrorists on the sidewalks, an un-latched baby-gate, an upturned pot of boiling water, a bicycle helmet forgotten... Only now do I think back to the girl who did not run and envy her ignorance of what could happen.

At the Threshold

by Scott Ruescher

It was all I could do, standing at the threshold of each
Softly lit gallery in the museum of Maya medicine
In San Cristóbal de las Casas, in this southern-most
Mexican state of Chiapas, to keep from jumping
The velvet rope, to suppress the surging, atavistic desire
To enter the astonishing diorama and surrender myself
To the depicted scene, taking my place among
The lifelike wax figures in one after another vignette
Of people in imaginable action—to join the life-sized,
Round-shouldered, black-haired indigenous women
Weaving wool clothing on looms in thatched huts,
Grinding maize on stone mortars, flipping tortillas
On rocks over pine-wood fires, and worshipping the gods
Of corn, rain, sunlight, and fertility with their husbands,
Their children, their extended families of grandparents
And cousins, on their hut's dirt floor, cushioned by a bed
Of fresh pine needles, like those we'd seen at the cathedral
On the *zócalo* in San Juan Chamula, where a priest
In a long white tunic, blessing a pregnant young woman,
Chanted a prayer in his staccato *Tuitil*, rolled an egg
Along her limbs, and wanded her with a full bottle
Of Coca-Cola, aglow in the light of hundreds of candles
Flickering in glass cups on the tile floor until
His cell phone rang and he excused himself for a minute—
Or not just to join but actually to be the man
In draw-string white pants and brown leather sandals,
Right about my size, someone I'm sure I could emulate,

His black hair square on his head, cutting firewood
In a clearing with a homemade axe, bare-chested and brown
As the man in the adjacent gallery thatching his hut
With palm leaves and lengths of vine, happy at last
To be as soft as that, no longer a man of blood and bone,
Hueso y carne, subject to all sorts of suffering, worried
About the world, or concerned about my reputation,
But content with my life, busy at last at the kind of hard work
That keeps you attached without twine to the earth.

The Noctambulist

by Leona Sevick

What dreams will make a child rise
from sleep and move about a
cold, dark house at two in the
morning? It took less than a
minute for my father to
wake, run from his bedroom to
the living room to switch off
the eight-track belting Marvin
Gaye at full blast. One by one,
he'd click off the lights I'd flicked
on, move to the kitchen where
I'd set the stand mixer on
high, left the toaster warming
a piece of phantom bread. I
picture my father groggy
with the sleep that my nightly
adventures deprived him of.
When all was safely unplugged,
he'd stumble back to the room
where I would be sitting straight-
backed and still on the sofa,
staring ahead at nothing
and no one. Gently he would
usher me back to my bed,
heeding the old words *don't wake
a walker*. Now, what wouldn't
I give to return to those

strange nights in my father's house,
to silence defeated by
brightness and vibration. To
trade these to-do lists, meeting
schedules, the mounting bills, these
damned pulsing anxieties
that cause me to rise at two
in the morning, open my
iPad and begin again
the hard work of drowning.

Witness

by Leona Sevick

I tell you I hardly know her, have spoken with her

a handful of times, mostly exchanging niceties

until we had to discuss the urgent, colder business

of leave days and coverage. Her husband—dead

after a week of symptoms, then surgery and follow-up.

At the service are the mother, two siblings and a handful

of close friends, my colleague and me, who knew the man

not at all. Sitting at the back of the room, listening obscenely

to the knotted details of a life, I am voyeur, interloper.

Deep into it now, I think of her returning to the home

bought three weeks before he'd begun acting strangely,

before he stopped at the red light two blocks too soon.

Confronted with unpacked boxes, with curtain rods

still on the floor, how will she find the will to dress?

Weeks later at work she will appear unchanged,

competent and capable. I will wonder at the

efforts expended to find matching shoes.

The Blue Shirt

by Susan Volchok

I take my book into the den along with my glass of wine and the bottle of pale nail polish I might do my toes with later. I don't feel like watching the stupid nature show my husband's watching. But I don't really want to read either. I'm not in the mood for anything. I'm not in much of a good mood at all.

My friend called this afternoon, about when I figured he would; the phone rang once and I picked up and said hello and he said hello, in the same soft but self-assured way, which told me we both knew we were expecting one another. We chatted for a little while about this and that; we often get together Thursdays for a few hours before I pick the twins up at school, which as it happens isn't until five on Thursday afternoons, and our schedules, his and mine, make Thursday a good choice for us, so after fifteen minutes or so of chat, I asked if he had any time. That's exactly how I put it: Do you have any time?

He said Yes, I have some time, right now, and it's so great being out, out of the house, I mean; I've been cooped up much too much all week.

Uh huh, I said, waiting for him to suggest that we get off the phone and he'd come on uptown. Or I could go down, since he'd added something about liking being there, meaning, where he was, midtown in a big building across the street from a fine vestpocket park. It's great there on a nice sunny day, which this is. Was. But he didn't seem to get it, my reference to having time, because he kept making small talk, hanging on the phone and after another little while, I cleared my throat and came out and asked him if he wanted to do something. That's what I meant about having time, I explained. Sorry, I guess I wasn't making myself clear. (Although it seemed to me he would've gotten it, just going by our past experience together on Thursdays, if he'd wanted to. You know?)

Well, he said. Ummm. What did you have in mind?

I don't know, I said, a walk. Or a bookstore. Or you could come over. Or I could meet you down there. Or part of the way down there, stop somewhere for a quick cup of something and—that's all.

Well, he said again. I don't know. To tell you the truth, I think I want to get back.

But he wasn't exactly telling the truth, or else why'd he just say what he said about being so happy to be sprung? I didn't say this in so many words, but I did point out the slight inconsistency: Not that you have to be consistent, I added. We laughed at that, for some reason. And I threw out a few more ideas for getting us together.

But he wasn't persuaded. I think I'd like to go for a run, if you want to know, he said; which was probably because we'd seen part of the marathon together Sunday last, and just now I'd teasingly mentioned a five-miler this coming Sunday I bet we could manage. I was supposed to find out more about it later on. At the moment, I suggested we each do a brisk walk, meet at the edge of the Park in a coffeehouse I'd taken him to a couple of times before, the last time being the day after his birthday last fall, when he let me buy him a piece of chocolate mousse cake to go with his usual single espresso.

Well, he said once more. I don't know. There was this tense little spot of silence. I was beginning to feel bad, then, because what did I need this for? I had work I could do; why offer to take time off to see a man who didn't want to see me? I stopped coming up with suggestions. And he finally admitted he didn't want to meet.

I don't know why, I just don't, he said.

It's okay, I said. And it was. He's having problems with his wife, for one thing, and he's paranoid about giving her anything else to hold over him, hate him for. Or so he's been saying. Whereas, for me, things are pretty cool at home, I can do pretty much what I want with my time. I don't, I mean, have to report in or anything, though personally I think it's a lot smarter to give a spouse the general impression they know what's doing in your life, instead of being squirrelly and strange about your comings and goings.

Anyway, just before we hung up I told him about a short story I'd read that I thought he'd like. In fact, it's a love story I'd like him to see because there's something about it that reminds me of—I don't know, I guess I just think he'd like it, that's all.

It's called "The Blue Shirt," I said, or "A Blue Shirt."

I'm wearing a blue shirt, he said.

Really, I said: *that* blue shirt? thinking of a dark denim one he'd recently shown up in, having uncharacteristically asked me over the phone that morning for advice about what to wear. And of course I'd admired it, maybe a little too enthusiastically.

But now he just said, Huh?

You know, I said, that shirt you were wearing.

Oh; no, he said, this is a different one. But you'd like it, it's a similar blue.

You're mean, then, I said (silly-sly, making myself smile) not coming over if you're wearing a blue shirt I'd like.

Hmm, he said. But that's as far as we went with that sort of thing.

Then I said, Well, maybe I'll send you the story if you can't find the book in the library. And that was it.

Afterward, I had to admit he probably had the right idea, staying away this Thursday. We saw each other twice last week—once (Thursday) his wife doesn't know about—and spoke every day for six days in a row. It's not that I was counting or anything, it's just something I realized, looking at my calendar this afternoon. We definitely needed a break and he's better at the detached, self-denying stuff than I am, which would explain why no calls five days after that streak, and no visit today. He knows exactly what he's doing. Meanwhile, I put in two more hours of work and felt hardly melancholy at all walking through the early November dusk to pick the boys up from their after-school soccer club.

Of course, it's true I told him this was their last soccer day, my last long Thursday until spring (or until I figure out something else), and also true that telling him didn't make any difference. But that probably only proves that he knew what needed doing better than I did.

Just as tonight, when I called to tell him what I'd gotten on the Road Runners Club tape about that race Sunday morning, and his wife answered, the usual curt hello, pass him the phone: he was brisk himself, as he has to be around her, and I was if anything even brisker, and it didn't seem to bother me, being businesslike instead of whatever I feel like being, which is almost anything but that. Still, it was all right, it was fine. At least, it was until this moment when, sitting here alone, with my book and etcetera, it suddenly struck me that I've pretty much made a fool of myself, and twice in one day. I can't even think now why I bothered, why I kept my voice so friendly, so warm it makes me a little sick thinking about it, comparing it with his coldness. Sick, and kind of sad too.

I don't even know whether I want to see him, and still, I go on being—just being there. I have no idea whether I do or do not want him to say, Yes I'll see you Sunday again, only this time the two of us sweating together instead of spectating. But I know he's going to say No, sorry, I can't, you know how it is, my schedule, Sundays. You know.

What he knows is that I hate when he uses his suspicious wife as an excuse. That I think it's nothing but bad faith. Let him take some responsibility for his choices. Like today. That was okay, even if he's not telling me the whole story. I don't really want to know anyway do I? He's going to say No. If he says yes, then I'll have to think about what *I* want to do. But it isn't going to happen. I don't have anything to worry about. Except it's eleven o'clock, the show's over in the bedroom, the news'll be blaring up any minute. Bed-time. It's funny, but the thing that bothers me the most is that when I told him I'd double checked the title of the story and it's actually just "The Shirt," not "The Blue Shirt," though it is about a blue shirt, he said Huh? again, then: What? And I'm not sure whether he was doing it for her benefit, or whether he'd really already for-gotten.

Lake Roland

by Dora Malech

2016

Lilacs, mown grass, and the scent of my own soap rising from the back of my neck in the heat. The train downtown sighs by beyond the trees. A minute later, the train into the county looks the other way. Fancy all these flowers opening to mouth their truest names. In a notebook from last spring: *I don't want Robert E. Lee Park to be this pretty.* It's spring again now, earth's orchestra pit swelling into green strains, vernal reprise. In between, nominal reprieve: in the fall, executives announced the park's new name—which had always been the name of the reservoir itself, actually—at the groundbreaking for a new nature center, ceremonial photo opportunity with hard hats, shovels, smiles. Re-placed. I visited the park for the first time last May, the month after what the city calls, alternately, the riots, the unrest, the uprising. The bill to rename was introduced last summer, later, following the Charleston shooting. I can't hear it, but there's music all around me—literally. Everyone walking and jogging past wears headphones, earbuds. Imagine hooks and bass lines, melodies unheard except for self-selecting audiences of one by one. Saying a thing's still slippery as the stones in the streambed of Roland Run. To say that we are listening is not to say that these are hearings, though there are hearings.

America: That Feeling When

by Dora Malech

full of suicide Coke

each gush released
in turn into one
white plastic chalice's
open mouth aimed wide
at heaven's fluorescent
fixtures' flickers
to receive

the syrup's sacrament
wild for to hold its aspartame

the super in superfluous
gulp runneth over in
alchemical union

each perfect bubble
bursting to be

ascendant in the straw
that's stiff and red
as a child's drawing
of her father's
hardened artery

you pull off to the side

of a back road beyond a town
where flags wave two
different flavors of anger

flapping simulacra
of the stars above

here in the headlights'
stripes of light
bars of light

as what's in
wants out and can't
wait any longer
for the next gas station
convenience store

you unzip and squat

to darken gravel dust
to ink blot test over which

you bend closer
toward a glint that turns
out to be your

stream shining
a spent shell casing

Flight Map

by Dora Malech

After Mohammed El-Kurd, Lily Sickles, et al.

It's just an in-class exercise. I ask
each student to share a line so we can
collaborate, weave disparate histories
together. It's just for fun, I say—a phrase
that probably sounds less than convincing
coming from the teacher, but no one
protests. Heads bowed, they put their pens to paper.
Mohammed writes of a refugeed God.
I ask if he means simply refugee
or maybe exiled and he says no, he knows
what he means is refugeed. Lily writes
her hair into the nests of birds on two
continents. Genetics twists her locks
to echoes of the double helixes
that make a home of each of us. My mind
flits to the pair of doves I saw startled
from what they'd built in the eaves, how verbs aver
agency, and how one might find that nest
and say it had been abandoned. We're moving
on, I say. I have a lesson prepared
on the first-person plural. I hit the arrow
on the PowerPoint. Soon, our session
will adjourn and we'll board our respective
flights back to New Jersey or to Moscow
or Jerusalem. Doves live on every

continent except the frozen poles.
Here's where I try to convince you
that we'll always have each other's words,
the holy nest in what's said honestly.

Shooting Pool

by Joshua Shapiro

*R*ack-em Billiards has sixteen tables, and it's set up so folks can stay out of other folks' way if they want to. As soon as the stranger walks in you have the feeling that what he wants is a little of the local scenery, and sure enough he sits down next to Cole. As if this isn't foolish enough he orders himself a margarita with a tequila the management doesn't stock and that the bartender, Bert, never heard of.

At the moment it's just you and Cole sitting with the stranger. Bert is polishing the taps that haven't poured beer in years. Over at one of the big Brunswick tables Archie is warming up. He's wearing the ostrich skin boots he says are for special occasions, and they have more tooling on them than the walnut stock of a .32 Winchester Special. But Archie's a little guy and you figure it's more about the advantage he gets shooting pool in those heels.

Rack-em's gets strangers occasionally, being about the only public place this side of town. Also there's a new server farm down the road. With land and taxes cheaper down here than just about anywhere, they've been popping up all over the state. Sure enough the stranger is from the server farm. Actually from the New York company that owns the farm, as he's quick to tell us.

You know what they do over there but decide to give the guy a little of what he came in for. You drawl, "Hey mister, what you raisin' on that there farm? Regular chickens or that special server kind?"

"I had that once," Cole says.

On the bar in front of Cole are what's left of a basket of crawfish and four empties. People here mostly drink Coors Silver Bullets when they're not drinking bourbon, and it's a little early for bourbon. Plus most of the guys want to stay sharp for the tournament. Sitting on the rail of Archie's table is a single beer, which you know is just for show. Archie will do anything to win, including stay dry. You're drinking your own Silver Bullet real slow, which is your style and doesn't get anybody to wondering. In fact you're only pretending to drink it. You want to make sure you're on top of your game too.

Cole doesn't shoot pool. Neither does Zane, who is exactly the kind of scenery that might interest the New Yorker. He's an old-timer who chews tobacco and spits wherever he wants. Maybe to show the stranger he can be civilized Zane spits into one of the ashtrays they still keep on the bar. He whines, "How's it I kin have a firearm in this place but I cain't have no cigarette?"

Bert behind the bar doesn't even look at Zane. You figure it's his way of saying he doesn't make the rules.

The stranger tells us his name is Grant. His designer glasses and sharp blazer say plain enough that he's not from around here. He takes a sip of his margarita. Floating in it are a couple of the lemon slices Bert leaves out day and night. Before Grant can say anything Archie comes over carrying his cue. He uses a McDermott Wildfire and the mother-of-pearl inlay on the barrel looks nice in the bar lights.

"Just so's you know," Archie says, clapping your arm but looking at Grant, "Hero Boy knows all about what goes on in that server farm of yours. Went to college, in fact."

"Where?" Grant asks.

"State," you say, about as concise as you figure this stranger expects. You don't want to leave the wrong impression so after a while you add, "But I don't have no degree or nothin'." You could say it with good English, but that would be part of the impression you don't want to leave.

Grant's glass is already empty and he signals Bert for another margarita. "And hold the lemons." Then he says to you, "I didn't believe for a minute you thought a server farm was agricultural."

"You tellin' me," Cole says in his slow way, "they don't raise no chickens?"

Grant smiles, not superior or anything, just what it looks like when there's one thing in your mind and something completely different in the other person's. Kind of how you've been feeling lately. Archie's whiskers move in a way that tells you he doesn't appreciate the out-of-towner's smile.

"Computers," Grant says. "Not chickens. It's interesting that most people don't get what a server farm actually does, even though they probably make use of one every day."

"And some people do get it," says Archie. "Matter of fact I dug the footings for your big ol' farm. And Hero Boy built the forms. He's just as good with a re-bar bender as he is with a pistol."

"Aw shucks," you say, still drawling like your granddaddy.

Archie gives you a tap on the arm with the butt end of his cue. He doesn't like it that you're putting on a down-home act, and his taps are the kind you still feel the next day.

Grant is looking at Archie's T-shirt. It's one of his gun shirts. This one says "All Those Opposed to the Right to Bear Arms Raise Your Hand!" Underneath are four people in a row. There's Hitler and Castro and Stalin, all with their hands raised. The last person in the row is Hillary. Real casual he asks, "Whereabouts in New York you from?"

"I live in Manhattan."

"Manhattan." Archie repeats the word like he's got one of Bert's lemon wedges in his mouth. "Maybe you can help me with somethin'. How is it that in New York a fella can't put more than seven rounds in his magazine?" Archie makes it his business to keep up with the laws even in states he's never visited.

"How many bullets do you think a gun should be allowed to hold?" Grant asks.

He says it easy but you can tell he's got an ax to grind. You have a feeling he knows this isn't the smartest place to grind it but doesn't care.

Old Zane spits again, this time not in the ashtray. "'Bout as many as a fella needs to protect hisself!"

You don't like the way the conversation is going and give Zane a look to shut him up. He's harmless but has a tendency to talk too much. Cole hardly talks unless he's had a few, and he's on his fifth. He puts a huge palm on the bar next to Grant's margarita and says, "I was on a hog shoot last week and wouldn't you know maybe a dozen them suckers come outta the woods. Emptied my thirty-round clip and most of another 'fore they run off."

"That's what I'm talkin' about!" says Archie. "Cole here might not of got him any hogs with one of your magazines. Tell Mister Manhattan how many hogs you got that day."

Cole tips his can back to get the last of the beer. He picks at the crumbs of his crawdads and wipes his mouth and doesn't say anything.

"See? That there's humility." Archie's leaning on the bar so his left side faces Grant. "Cole's been busy freezin' hog meat all week and he won't even tell us how much."

Archie's turned the way he is so Grant can get a look at his holster. It's black stitched leather, and in it is his Ruger SR9. Since open carry a few of the boys have started wearing theirs but no-body more regular than Archie. Grant pretends he doesn't see the gun. But he does, since the whole point is you can't not see it. The New Yorker takes off his blazer and loosens his tie.

You've seen his kind before, not in this place but on campus, where half the people seemed to be looking for trouble. Or maybe they were so full of ideas they couldn't stop themselves. You were there for only a semester before your money ran out, but your eyes got opened to a few things. One is how an idea can be as dangerous as a gun.

It's starting to get busy, the way it always does before a tour-nament. There's no stools left at the bar and everyone is pressed in close. The New Yorker doesn't seem to mind. He turns to Cole, inches away, and says, "This is fascinating. How many of those hogs *did* you shoot?"

You can see Cole getting uncomfortable. His big body is bent over and his eyes are closed.

"Go on, answer the man," Archie says. "He come all this way so he could take home some good redneck stories."

Up to this point the general tone has been like one of Archie's taps, hard but playful. Now, unless a person knows Archie it's im-possible to tell when he stops being one thing and starts being an-other, so you can't blame this Grant for not realizing how the con-versation is starting to turn.

Cole unbends a little and says into his beer, "Didn't shoot none of 'em."

Zane gives his best backwoods hoot. The inside of his mouth looks like a fresh dug post hole. Somebody hoping to see the sights could hardly do better, but the New Yorker doesn't seem interested.

Archie says, "You meanin' to tell me you was out there with

your Bushmaster and a couple thirty-round mags and you didn't hit one of them hogs? Jeez, Cole, what's Mister Manhattan here gonna think? You givin' us rednecks a bad name."

"That word," Grant says. "It's your word, not mine."

Archie touches the pointy tip of one of his ostrich boots to the New Yorker's shin. "But you was thinkin' it."

"Actually, I was thinking that thirty bullets in a gun might sound reasonable when you're out hunting." Grant adjusts his glasses like he wants to see better what he's gotten himself into. Then he goes on. "But aren't we talking about the same sort of weapon that's used in all these massacres? A gun that shoots as fast as you can pull the trigger? Correct me if I'm wrong."

"What y'all think? Does Mister Manhattan here need correctin'?"

There's some quiet sipping and shifting about.

"Let Hero Boy here do the correctin'!" Zane shouts. His thumbs are hooked under his suspenders. "He's a sharpshooter!"

It was your army job for two years, in Iraq. But you keep quiet. You used to have an opinion that was pretty much the opinion of everybody you know, but that was before college. Also before the IED on a Fallujah street. The fact is, you've been doing some thinking. You do it when you're behind Archie's house putting rounds through man-sized targets at two hundred yards. You do it when you cluster your shots in a circle no bigger than a human heart. You do it when Archie says you're the one he wants with him if the Feds ever come. And they're coming, about that he's sure. All this time you're thinking there's something crazy going on when anybody can own just about anything, and crazy is exactly what folks sometimes get.

Of course you never say this out loud, just like there's lots of things you never say out loud in these parts. Now here's this New Yorker saying them.

"Actually, I believe I've got my facts right. It's simple, really. We have more guns than any other civilized country. So we have more gun deaths. Not just a few more, ten or twenty times. In some cases a hundred times. Other societies look at us and can't comprehend it. Neither can I or most of the people I know."

All the clicking from the tables has stopped. Bert is just standing behind the bar with a dish towel in his hands. The loudest sound is the crumpling of Cole's beer can. You've seen guys get on Archie's bad side before. The way Grant is going he stands a chance of having about as many teeth left at the end of the night as Zane, if he's that lucky. But you're not about to stop him because you want to hear more. You want everyone to hear.

Things don't work out that way, though. What's going to happen happens right then, fast like it always does, except instead of Archie it's Cole. He's sitting all hunched and inside himself one moment and the next is holding the New Yorker's tie up by the knot.

"Show him a little hardware," Zane yells at you. He's bouncing on his stool and popping his suspenders against his skinny chest, chaw juice drooling from his lower lip. "Show'em your Double Eagle! Show'em your .357!" But everyone's looking at the stranger.

"You don't come in here insultin' our ways!" Cole says, holding tight to the tie.

Grant is in no position to say anything, but you notice his eyes. There's no fear in them. Then Archie does something nobody expects. He gets friendly.

"How 'bout easin' up on Mister Manhattan, Cole. Give the man a chance to say what he came here to say. Show him we're as fair-minded as other folk."

Cole follows Archie like the rest of us and lets go of the tie. Grant does some catching up on his breathing, then he sort of does say what you were hoping he would.

"I'm not trying to offend any of you. In fact, we've got a lot in common. When somebody shoots up a school I know you're as horrified as I am. You just have a different idea about how to stop it. That would be more guns, not fewer, but in the hands of the right people. People who understand the weapons. People who know how to use them wisely. Good people. In other words, people like yourselves." He lets this sit with everybody as if it's a piece of flattery, which you know it isn't. Then he adds, with the same smile that got under Cole's skin, "People who can shoot straight."

He doesn't look at Cole and doesn't have to. The boys at the bar and even the ones who stopped playing pool laugh. Archie laughs. Nobody seems to mind the guy having his fun after what Cole did to him. Bert looks relieved that he won't be sweeping up any teeth. They all respect somebody who mans up, and probably Archie saw the same courage in the guy's eyes you did.

"That's puttin' it kinda pretty for my taste," says Archie, "but you got it about right. Start takin' away our guns and the only ones that'll have 'em are on the wrong side of the law. And the wackos."

"The wackos!" Zane howls.

Grant says, "Nobody's talking about taking away your guns."

"Then what the hell you talkin' about?" says Archie.

"Reasonable restrictions."

Archie points at his T-shirt. "Only kind of restrictions I understand."

This seems to settle it for the New Yorker. Not that he looks either persuaded or scared, just worn down. He stands up and takes out a twenty and lays it on the bar. The second margarita in front of him is still full.

"Sure you don't wanna stay a spell?" says Archie, waving his cue at the busy tables. "Tournament's about to start. It's the biggest event we got next to the county fair."

"Some other time." Grant puts on his jacket. "I've got a plane to catch. One last question though."

Archie's whiskers move again in that unpredictable way. "I thought we was all done with that. But what the hell. Shoot." For effect he reaches for his holster but what he aims at Grant is only a finger.

"You say you want guns in the hands of the good guys. The people who aren't, as you put it, wackos."

"What's your point?"

"My point is—" Grant's eyes go to the pool tables and to the gun on Archie's hip and to the men at the bar. He seems to look extra hard at you, and you need to remind yourself how these days you sometimes imagine things. Then he says, more sad than argumentative, "My point is that people aren't always what they seem."

It would be a good way to end things, but as usual Archie has the last word. "You see, that's the difference between your neck of the woods and ours. Folks down here just know each other."

There was a time when you would have agreed with Archie. But it's a technology world, and the server farm is humming night and day, and you understand about as well as the next person how to use a computer. It doesn't take more than a little looking around online to realize people are hard to figure.

"Talkin's over," Zane says when the visitor is gone. "Talkin' ain't worth a damn. That boy wasn't changin' any minds with his talkin'. It's tournament time!"

You don't even bother telling Zane to quiet down. You know nobody hears him. The tourist who comes in thinking it might be interesting to meet a real hillbilly doesn't even see him. His own kind don't see him. He's too ornery or too ridiculous or maybe too true. At least that's what the VA doctors have been telling you.

You aren't one of those glory seekers but you do wonder what folks will say. Mentally ill is the term the TV people like to throw around, but you don't think you're that. At least not the part of you who needs to express his views, like everyone does. You just go about it in your own way.

Archie's Ruger handled so well you went out and bought one. It's gun number thirty-three. The Ruger and two Glocks and the Kel-Tek with the folding stock are all in your cue case. There's also five thirty-round magazines for the rifle, and as many fifteen-rounders for the handguns as you could fit. You don't figure on needing the long gun, though. You have the advantage of knowing who carries and who doesn't. Bert keeps a six-shot Colt behind the bar.

Acknowledgements

"**Crossing Nguyễn Du Street**" from *Said Not Said* ©2017 by Fred Marchant Published by Graywolf Press. Used with permission.

Contributors

Alex Ahmed is a PhD student in the Personal Health Informatics program at Northeastern University. She is also a union organizer, working on improving the working conditions of graduate student employees. In her spare time she sings in an a capella group called the Kinsey Scales, plays guitar and board games, and obsesses about Star Trek. She can be found on Twitter @WomensFormula.

Claire Chafee is a playwright and a teacher. She holds an MFA from Brown University and an MA from Harvard in Arts Education. Her play, "Why We Have a Body" opened at The Magic Theatre in San Francisco (1993) where it ran for 7 months, winning her the Dramalogue Award, the Bay Area Critic's Circle Award and *New York Newsday's* Oppenheimer Award. It was produced Off-Broadway by The Women's Project in NYC. It is published in *Women Playwrights: the Best Plays of 1993* (Smith and Krauss) and *The Actors Book of Gay and Lesbian Plays* (Penguin). Her plays have been produced in San Francisco, New York, Minneapolis and elsewhere and have won numerous awards including the Jane Chambers Award in 2013 for FULL/SELF. She has taught graduate creative writing at SF State and California College of the Arts and recently moved with her family to Cambridge. A previous essay, "The Algebra of Buried Things" was published in Harvard's *Ed. Magazine*. She also writes fiction.

Maryann Corbett spent almost thirty-five years working for the Office of the Revisor of Statutes at the Minnesota Legislature. Her work has appeared in journals like *32 Poems, Barrow Street, Ecotone, Rattle, River Styx, Southwest Review,* and *Subtropics* and in anthologies like *The Best American Poetry 2018* and *Measure for Measure: An Anthology of Poetic Meters*. Her third book, *Mid Evil*, won the 2014 Richard Wilbur Award; she is also a past winner of the Willis Barnstone Translation Prize and a past finalist for the Howard Nemerov Sonnet Award. Her fourth book, *Street View*, was a finalist for the Able Muse Book Prize and was published in 2017 by Able Muse Press.

Lâle Davidson, a recent winner of the SUNY Chancellor's Award for Excellence in Scholarship and Creative Activity, teaches writing at the SUNY Adirondack in upstate New York. In addition to her own blog site, *A Writing Life*, she blogs for *Luna Station Quarterly*. Her stories have appeared in *The North American Review*, *Eclectica*, *Big Lucks*, and *The Collagist*. Her fabulist story "The Opal Maker" was named top fifty of 2015 by *Wigleaf*, and her fiction chapbook, *Strange Appetites* won the Adirondack Center for Writing People's Choice Award in 2016.

Diane Fiedler is a fine artist, designer, illustrator and art educator. Her illustration, design & exhibition design clients include Fidelity Investments, Astra-Zeneca, Fisons Pharmaceuticals, Gillette, MIT, The Broad Institute, Harvard, Harcourt Brace, and The Boston Children's Museum for educational exhibits, greeting cards, early readers, magazines, college textbooks, webisodes, and EdX courses. She has taught Sci-Art classes at Tufts Experimental College/SMFA, Boston. Fiedler's giant watercolors have been floated and photographed in Arctic glacial waters by expeditions of the Royal Canadian Geographic Society and exhibited at the Explorer's Club in New York.

Heather June Gibbons is the author of the poetry collection *Her Mouth as Souvenir*, winner of the 2017 Agha Shahid Ali Poetry Prize from the University of Utah Press, and two chapbooks, *Sore Songs* and *Flyover*. A graduate of the University of Iowa Writers' Workshop, she teaches creative writing at San Francisco State University and in the community. She lives in San Francisco.

Max Heinegg's poems have appeared in *The Cortland Review*, *Columbia Poetry Review*, *Tar River Poetry*, *December Magazine*, and *Crab Creek Review*, among others. Additionally, he is a singer-songwriter and recording artist, and the co-founder and brewmaster of Medford Brewing Company. He lives and teaches English in the public schools of Medford, MA.

Lynn Holmgren's poetry and prose have appeared in *Stoneboat Journal*, *Glassworks Magazine*, *Belletrist*, *The Cape Cod Poetry Review*, *Ocean State Review*, and elsewhere. Her poem "Girl with Cherries (Copley Square)" was nominated for a Pushcart Prize. She earned an MFA in fiction from UMass Boston and has organized a number of storytelling events including "Edible Stories" and Boston's first "Human Library". She lives in Jamaica Plain with her husband and their two cats, Matcha and Earl Gray.

Cory Hutchinson-Reuss grew up in Arkansas and holds a PhD in English from the University of Iowa. Her poems have appeared in journals such as *The Pinch, Drunken Boat, Four Way Review, Salamander, Witness*, and in *Crazyhorse* for the 2016 Lynda Hull Memorial Prize for Poetry. She is a 2017 Best New Poets nominee and a poetry reader for *The Adroit Journal*. She lives in Iowa City.

Joseph Johnson teaches in New Meadows, Idaho. He received his MFA from the University of Massachusetts-Amherst, and his work has appeared or is forthcoming in *Big Big Wednesday; Chicago Review; Forklift, Ohio; Pleiades; Yalobusha Review; and elsewhere.*

Judy Kessler abandoned her role as Knowledge Architect (aka technical writer) to write fiction. A native of Detroit and proud graduate of the University of Michigan, she is a long-time Boston area resident. In 2017, her story "Falling Season" won *Arkana's* first prize for fiction. She hopes that someday her novel-in-progress reaches as global an audience as her guides for software developers and tech writers.

Vera Kroms lives and writes in Boston, MA. She has degrees in mathematics and has worked as a programmer for many years. Her chapbook *Necessary Harm* was published by Finishing Line Press. Her poems have appeared in *Tupelo Quarterly, Gulf Coast, Colombia Journal of the Arts, Southern Poetry Review* and others.

Kendra Stanton Lee strives for equanimity by editing punctuation errors she sees out in the wild. She lives in Milton, MA at a boarding school that provides all her meals and ample writing material. She lives alongside 300 teenagers, her cute husband, their relentlessly funny tween children, and one wily dog. Find her online at http://www.kendrastantonlee.com.

Dora Malech is the author of *Stet*, selected by Susan Stewart for the Princeton Series of Contemporary Poets and published by Princeton University Press in 2018. Her two previous books of poetry are *Say So* (Cleveland State University Poetry Center, 2011) and *Shore Ordered Ocean* (The Waywiser Press, 2009), and her fourth book, *Flourish*, is forthcoming from Carnegie Mellon University Press in 2020. Her poems have appeared in publications that include *The New Yorker*, *Poetry*, *The Best American Poetry*, *Poetry London*, *The Kenyon Review*, *Lana Turner*, and *Tin House*. Her visual art has appeared or is forthcoming in publications that include *Poetry*, *Poetry Northwest*, and *Pinwheel*. She is the recipient of awards that include an Amy Clampi Residency Award from the Amy Clampi Foundation, a Writers' Fellowship from the Civitella Ranieri Foundation, a Ruth Lilly Poetry Award from the Poetry Foundation, and a Mary Sawyers Baker Award from the William G. Baker, Jr. Memorial Fund. She lives in Baltimore, Maryland, where she is an assistant professor in The Writing Seminars at Johns Hopkins University.

Angelo Mao is a biomedical engineering research scientist in the Boston area. He obtained his Ph.D. from Harvard University in 2017. His poems have appeared in *New American Writing*, *Lana Turner*, *Denver Quarterly*, *Nat Brut*, and elsewhere.

Fred Marchant is the author of five books of poetry, the most recent of which is *Said Not Said* (2017). Earlier books include *The Looking House*, *Full Moon Boat*, and *House on Water, House in Air*. His first book, *Tipping Point*, won the 1993 Washington Prize, and was reissued in a 20th anniversary second edition. Marchant has co-translated works by Vietnamese poets Tran Fang Khoa and Vo Que. He has also edited *Another World Instead: The Early Poems of William Stafford*. An emeritus professor of English, he is the winner of the May Sarton Award from the New England Poetry Club, given to poets "whose work is an inspiration to to other writers."

Jennifer Martelli is the author of *My Tarantella* (Bordighera Press), as well as the chapbook, *After Bird* (Grey Book Press, winner of the open reading, 2016). Her work has appeared in *Verse Daily*, *The Bitter Oleander*, and *Iron Horse Review* (winner, Photo Finish contest). She is the recipient of the Massachusetts Cultural Council Grant in Poetry. She is the co-poetry editor for *The Mom Egg Review*.

Deborah Norkin is the Food Writing Editor for *Pangyrus*. Her features, essays and fiction have appeared in magazines and newspapers, including *The Boston Globe*. She lives in the Boston area where she produces and hosts author and literary events. Please visit her website, events page, and blog at DeborahNorkin.com.

Line Olsson is an independent cartoonist from Norway. She now lives in Brookline, Massachusetts, where she is a member of the cartoonist collective, the Boston Comics Roundtable. She has published comics in various anthologies, and has collaborated with other comic creators on longer publications. Her signature black and white line art has appeared in a variety of media. Most notably, she was the illustrator for the Emmy-nominated documentary film, American Denial--which aired on PBS's American Lens--in 2015. Line creates an ongoing journal-type cartoon series, under the title Out of Line. Her independent publications include *Dog Sea Son* (2010) and *Happy Hour in the Temple of Love* (2017). She is currently working on a graphic novel. www.lineolsson.com

Jennifer Packard is the author of *A Taste of Broadway: Food in Musical Theater*. She holds an MBA from the Wharton School and a Masters of Liberal Arts in Gastronomy from Boston University. Jennifer has nearly twenty years of experience working in marketing in the food industry. She also loves to make up new recipes which she tests out on her husband and three teen-aged sons.

Erin Pushman's work has appeared or is forthcoming in *The Gettysburg Review, Confrontation, Segue, Pangyrus, 1966: a Journal of Creative Nonfiction, Breastfeeding Today, Cold Mountain Review, Writing on the Edge, Women's Health Today, More New Monologues for Women by Women II* (Heinemann), *Boomtown* (Pres 53), *WAVES* (ARAHO), and elsewhere. Her book, *Reading as a Writer: Ten Lessons to Elevate Your Reading and Writing Practice*, is forthcoming from Bloomsbury Academic in 2021. She is currently revising a memoir about the women in her family learning to live in compromised bodies and blogging about her daughter's battle with a disfiguring disease at https://thefaceofbravery.wordpress.com/. The recipient of a 2017 North Carolina Regional Artist Project Grant, she is an English professor at Limestone College, where she directs the Writing Center.

Benoît Rey is a scientific journalist. He studied physics and chemistry in Lille, France, and then entered at the Ecole Superieure de Journalisme de Lille to study one year of scientific journalism. He has been a freelance scientific journalist for 12 years now, writing in French science magazines, most of the time about physics and astrophysics.

Scott Ruescher published his 2017 book, *Waiting for the Light to Change*, with Prolific Press. Some of the poems in the book won annual prizes from *Able Muse, Poetry Quarterly*, and the New England Poetry Club, and others appeared in *Agni, Ploughshares, Shadowgraph Quarterly, Common Ground Review*, and many other journals. He has been reading at various venues in the Boston area, including Gallery 263, the Somerville Armory, the Aeronaut Brewery (for Porter Square Books), the Newton Free Library, and the Cambridge Arts River Festival, and has been contributing new poems to *About Place, Tower Journal, Evening Street Review, Muddy River Poetry Review, Intima: A Journal of Narrative Medicine, Solstice,* and *Ohio Today,* the alumni magazine of his undergrad alma mater, Ohio University. In a blurb on the back of *Waiting for the Light to Change,* the late great Tony Hoagland called him "an evangelist for reality, declaiming its glitzy multitudinosity in long cinematic sentences."

Eliezra Schaffzin's fiction has most recently appeared in *Conjunctions, Salt Hill,* and *SmokeLong Quarterly*'s 15th-anniversary contest issue. She is a recipient of the Calvino Prize, awarded for a work of fiction written in the fabulist experimentalist style of Italo Calvino. Links to her published and performed stories, essays, and texts for music are curated at eliezraschaffzin.com.

Leona Sevick's work appears in *The Journal, Crab Orchard Review, The Normal School, The Southeast Review, The Arkansas International,* and other journals. Her work also appears in *The Golden Shovel Anthology: New Poems Honoring Gwendolyn Brooks* (Univ. of Arkansas Press, 2017, forward by Terrance Hayes). She is the 2017 *Press 53* Poetry Award Winner for her first full-length book of poems, *Lion Brothers.* Sevick was named a Tennessee Williams Scholar for the 2018 Sewanee Writers' Conference. She teaches Asian American literature at Bridgewater College, and she can be reached at leonasevick.com.

Joshua Shapiro's short fiction has appeared in *Beloit Fiction Journal, G.W. Review, Literary Review, Straylight, Phoebe, The Main Street Rag* and *The Write Place at the Write Time.* He is the author of the novel *Beautiful Before the Fall.* He's been a carpenter, an engineer, a teacher, and a musician. He has degrees from SUNY-Albany and Harvard, and is an alumni of the Bread Loaf Writers Conference. He lives outside Boston with his wife and daughter.

Mike Sinert is a freelance writer and essayist. A one-time daily newspaper reporter, he worked in technology marketing and public relations for two decades. Mike is a graduate of the Memoir Incubator at Boston's GrubStreet creative writing center. He was a general contributor at the 2017 Bread Loaf Writers' Conference and a 2017 fellow at the Virginia Center for Creative Arts. He also held a one-year fellowship in nonfiction at the Writers' Room of Boston. His memoir-in-progress, *Stuffed: All the Things I Ate and Why*, is one man's story of a 20-year, life and almost-death struggle with binge eating disorder. An excerpt appeared in *The Rumpus*. He holds an MBA from Northeastern University and lives near Boston.

Marley Stuart is an Assistant Editor of *Louisiana Literature* and a graduate of the Bennington Writing Seminars. His stories and poems have recently appeared or are forthcoming in *The Chattahoochee Review, Permafrost, Painted Bride Quarterly, Backstory, SPEAK The Magazine*, and elsewhere. He and his wife, the writer Kimberly Dawn Stuart, live in New Orleans and direct the small press River Glass Books.

Dariel Suarez was born and raised in Havana, Cuba. He immigrated to the United States with his family in 1997, during the island's economic crisis known as The Special Period. He is the author of the novel *The Playwright's House* (forthcoming, Red Hen Press) and the story collection *A Kind of Solitude* (Willow Springs Books), winner of the 2017 Spokane Prize for Short Fiction. Dariel is an inaugural City of Boston Artist Fellow and the Director of Core Programs and Faculty at GrubStreet. His prose has appeared or is forthcoming in numerous publications, including *The Threepenny Review, The Kenyon Review, Prairie Schooner, Michigan Quarterly Review, The Massachusetts Review, Southern Humanities Review*, and *The Caribbean Writer*, where his work was awarded the First Lady Cecile de Jongh Literary Prize. Dariel earned his M.F.A. in Fiction at Boston University and now resides in the Boston area with his wife and daughter.

Marjorie Thomsen is the author of the poetry collection, *Pretty Things Please* (Turning Point, 2016). She has been nominated twice for a Pushcart Prize and Best of the Net. Her poems have received awards and have been read on The Writer's Almanac. A poem about hiking in a dress and high heels was made into a short animated film as part of the ARTS By The People/Moving Words project. In 2018, she completed certification training through Mass Poetry and Lesley University to become a poet in residence in the Boston public schools and elsewhere. Marjorie serves on the board of the New England Poetry Club and is a clinical social worker.

Susan Volchok is a New York writer who has published widely in journals and anthologies, in mainstream magazines and newspapers, including *The New York Times*, and online at numerous sites including *n+1, The Common, The Literary Bohemian* and *Pangyrus* (this is her second appearance here.) Her website is http://www.susanvolchok.com

Guinotte Wise's work has appeared in numerous journals including *Atticus*, *Rattle*, *Ekphrastic Review*, *The MacGuffn*, and *Southern Humanities Review*. His first short story collection (*Night Train, Cold Beer*) won publication by a university press and enough money to fix the soffits. A 5-time Pushcart nominee, he writes and welds steel sculpture on a farm in Southeast Kansas. His latest book of poetry, *Horses See Ghosts*, was published in April, 2018. His book of essays, *Chickens One Day, Feathers the Next* will be published in July, 2019. Some work is at http://www.wisesculpture.com

Vincent Yu is an employee and shareholder of W.W. Norton. He graduated from Yale University, where he was a staff member of the *Yale Literary Magazine*. When not supporting the work of other writers, he dedicates his efforts to making his own. His work has appeared or is forthcoming in *Adelaide Magazine*, *Sierra Nevada Review*, *Cold Creek Review*, and *Able Muse*. He is represented by Natalie Grazian of Martin Literary Management.

ABOUT PANGYRUS

Pangyrus is a Boston-based group of writers, editors, and artists with a new vision for how high-quality creative work can prosper online and in print. We aim to foster a community of individuals and organizations dedicated to art, ideas, and making culture thrive.

Combining Pangaea and gyrus, the terms for the world continent and whorls of the cerebral cortex crucial to verbal association, Pangyrus is about connection.

INDEX by AUTHOR

www.ingramcontent.com/pod-product-compliance
Lightning Source LLC
Chambersburg PA
CBHW020618120726
47905CB00003B/843